D. H. LAWRENCE

A BEGINNER'S GUIDE

D. H. LAWRENCE

A BEGINNER'S GUIDE

JENNY WEATHERBURN
Series Editors
Rob Abbott & Charlie Bell

Hodder & Stoughton

A MEMBER OF THE HODDER HEADLINE GROUP

Orders: please contact Bookpoint Ltd, 130 Milton Park, Abingdon, Oxon OX14 4SB. Telephone: (44) 01235 827720, Fax: (44) 01235 400454. Lines are open from 9.00–6.00, Monday to Saturday, with a 24-hour message answering service. Email address: orders@bookpoint.co.uk

British Library Cataloguing in Publication Data
A catalogue record for this title is available from The British Library

ISBN 0 340 80378 9

First published 2001
Impression number 10 9 8 7 6 5 4 3 2 1
Year 2007 2006 2005 2004 2003 2002 2001

Cover photo by Corbis
Cover illustration by Jacey
Illustrations by Steve Coots
Typeset by Transet Limited, Coventry, England.
Printed in Great Britain for Hodder & Stoughton Educational, a division of Hodder Headline Plc, 338 Euston Road, London NW1 3BH by Cox & Wyman, Reading, Berks.

CONTENTS

How to use this book

The *Beginner's Guide* series aims to introduce readers to major writers of the past 500 years. It is assumed that readers will begin with little or no knowledge and will want to go on to explore the subject in other ways.

BEGIN READING THE AUTHOR

This book is a companion guide to D. H. Lawrence's major works, it is not a substitute for reading the books themselves. It would be useful if you read some of the works in parallel, so that you can put theory into practice. This book is divided into sections. After considering how to approach the author's work and a brief biography, we go on to explore some of Lawrence's main writings and themes before examining some critical approaches to the author. The survey finishes with suggestions for further reading and possible areas of further study.

HOW TO APPROACH UNFAMILIAR OR DIFFICULT TEXTS

Coming across a new writer may seem daunting, but do not be put off. The trick is to persevere. Much good writing is multi-layered and complex. It is precisely this diversity and complexity which makes literature rewarding and exhilarating.

Literature often needs to be read more than once and in different ways. These ways can include: a leisurely and superficial reading to get the main ideas and narrative; a slower more detailed reading focusing on the nuances of the text, concentrating on what appear to be key passages; and reading in a random way, moving back and forth through the text to examine such things as themes, or narrative or characterization. Every reader has an individual approach but undoubtedly the best way to extract the most from a text is to read it several times.

In complex texts it may be necessary to read in short chunks. When it comes to tackling difficult words or concepts it is often enough to guess in context on the first reading, making a more detailed study using a dictionary or book of critical concepts on later reading. If you prefer to look up unusual words as you go along, be careful that you do not disrupt the flow of the text and your concentration.

VOCABULARY

You will see that keywords and unfamiliar words are set in **bold** text. These words are defined and explained in the glossary to be found at the back of the book. In order to help you further we have also included a summary at the end of each chapter.

You can read this introductory guide in its entirety or dip in wherever suits you. You can read it in any order. This book is a tool to help you appreciate a key figure in literature. We hope you enjoy reading it and find it useful.

✱ ✱ ✱ *SUMMARY* ✱ ✱ ✱

To maximise the use of this book:

- read the author's work

- read it several times in different ways

- be open to innovative or unusual forms of writing

- persevere.

Rob Abbott & Charlie Bell

Why read Lawrence today?

HARDY'S CONTEMPORARY

We think of Lawrence, today, as a writer in the spirit of the modern age. Yet he was actually born into the gas-lit Victorian epoch in 1885. Dickens had died only 15 years before his birth. Lawrence's mother did not expect him to survive; he was a sickly child and subject to frequent bouts of ill-health throughout his life. He died at the age of only 44 in 1930. Thomas Hardy, a much longer-lived author, pre-deceased him by only two years.

BORN AHEAD OF HIS TIME

To his contemporaries, D. H. Lawrence was an extremely controversial figure: it seems to us now, with the benefit of hindsight, that in common with some other geniuses, he was born ahead of his time. In his own life-time his life-style, ideas and work provoked endless criticism. His views were vilified and ridiculed; his poetry was censored; his novels were given largely hostile reviews. *The Rainbow* was prosecuted for obscenity in 1915 and at the trial his publishers expressed remorse for ever publishing it in the first place. The magistrate ordered all copies to be seized and burned. Just over ten years later Lawrence's London publisher refused to print even an expurgated version of *Lady Chatterley's Lover*; Lawrence had to publish it privately in Italy. Even an exhibition of Lawrence's paintings was raided by police, who seized many canvases. When he and his wife tried to live quietly in Cornwall during the First World War, they were regarded with such a degree of distrust that they were suspected of spying, had their home searched by police and were forced to leave the county.

AN INNOVATOR

In what ways was he an innovator who succeeded in making his contemporaries so uncomfortable, and why was he so misunderstood?

Well, sex is a straightforward, simple answer, but of course not the whole one. Certainly every author writing after Lawrence was influenced by the original way in which he dealt with sexual relationships.

Lawrence was very aware of himself as a catalyst for change, of his efforts to try to do something very new with the spirit and content of the novel. His ideas are ones which naturally strike a sympathetic chord with modern readers and more often he conveys them vividly, memorably and with extraordinary sensitivity. He wrote, 'My field is to know the feelings inside a man, and make new feelings conscious.' ('The State of Funk', from *Selected Essays*).

A MODERN CONSCIOUSNESS

Few writers can better Lawrence in writing so movingly about the finest nuances of feeling in relationships. He recognized that a relationship is never static: 'Love is not a goal; it is only a travelling' ('Love', from *Selected Essays*) and that a thoroughly satisfying, mutually supportive and rewarding relationship is the highest attainable good:

> You mustn't think that your desire or your fundamental need is to make a good career, or to fill your life with activity, or even to provide for your family materially. It isn't. Your most vital necessity in this life is that you shall love your wife completely and implicitly and in entire nakedness of body and spirit. Then you will have peace and inner security, no matter how many things go wrong.
>
> (*Selected Letters*)

He also championed a belief in the overriding importance of gut-instinct as opposed to rationality: 'We can go wrong in our minds. But what our blood feels and believes and says is always true' (*Selected Letters*). Yet another way in which his attitudes seem now so in tune with our own is his awareness of the repressive, dead influence of materialism. He talked of the 'horrible ... insatiable struggle and desire to possess' (*Selected Letters*) – and the creeping, corrosive force of industrialization.

LIVING IN THE NOW

Another way in which Lawrence seems strongly in accord with modern feeling is his sense of the importance of living in the now – and getting the most out of every moment. This was an aspect of the man particularly valued and appreciated by those who knew him. It probably came, in part, from genetic inheritance: it was the aspect of his father which most drew and attracted his mother in the early days of their courtship. But it would have been accentuated, perhaps, by the frailty of his health: when you have been ill so many times, you tend to have a strong sense of the need to make the very most of the times you are well. In *Apocalypse* he wrote: 'For man, the vast marvel is to be alive. For man, as for flower, beast and bird, the supreme triumph is to be most vividly, most perfectly alive ... We ought to dance with rapture that we should be alive and in the flesh, and part of the living, incarnate cosmos.' Part of the joy of reading Lawrence is his ability to render fresh, alive and quite unforgettable whatever it is he wishes us to see – whether flowers, creatures, places or people.

SENSUOUS WRITING

This brings us on to the fact of Lawrence being a master of vivid, sensuous description which stays in the mind long after reading the page. Who, after reading the poem 'Kangaroo', could ever after see the animal except in terms of her 'beautiful slender face', her 'little loose hands, and drooping Victorian shoulders', 'the great muscular python-stretch of her tail' and the 'long flat skis of her legs'? Then there is his description of a tree-heather in 'Flowery Tuscany' (*Selected Essays*):

> it grows sometimes as tall as a man, lifting up its spires and its shadowy-white fingers with a ghostly fullness, amid the dark, rusty green of its lower bushiness; and it gives off a sweet honeyed scent in the sun, and a cloud of fine white stone-dust, if you touch it.

These are treasures indeed for a reader to keep for ever.

✳ ✳ ✳*SUMMARY*✳ ✳ ✳

Lawrence is relevant to us today because of:

- his importance as an innovator

- his attitudes to relationships and his ability to evoke the finest nuances of feeling

- his interesting and 'modern' ideas

- his sensitive use of language, particularly in descriptive or symbolic passages.

How to approach Lawrence's work

By looking at Lawrence's short story 'The White Stocking' and his poem 'Snake', we can get a shrewd sense of what to expect from this particular writer both in the sense of his style and his preoccupations.

'THE WHITE STOCKING'

Here we have a couple confronting a crisis two years into their marriage – the same point in time at which Lydia and Tom Brangwen experience the watershed of their marriage in *The Rainbow*. The time-span of the crisis is during one day, although Lawrence interpolates the main narrative with details of particular events which took place just over two years ago and later in order to make subsequent attitudes and reactions clear.

At the beginning of the story, the young wife, Elsie, leaps out of bed with unaccustomed alacrity on the morning of Valentine's Day: she is eagerly anticipating a gift from a current admirer who was her former employer, Sam Adams. She expects the gift to be both expensive and provocative – and it is: pearl earrings wrapped in a white stocking. She knows she will need to invent a story to explain away her acquisition of the earrings and decides 'she would pretend she had inherited them from her grandmother'. However, in the end she can't resist taunting her young husband with the truth about the gift; she wants him to realize how desirable she is in the eyes of other men. He is, predictably, beside himself with fury.

Typical features to note in this story

Although the couple have been married two years, they each experience great joy in the other's physicality. Lawrence conveys this kind of delight brilliantly and one is reminded of Will and Anna's honeymoon in *The Rainbow*. Elsie enjoys watching her young husband wash himself – just as Lawrence describes his own delight in the poem

'Gloire de Dijon' and Connie's when she watches Mellors in *Lady Chatterley's Lover*:

> As she whisked about, clearing the table, she loved the way in which he stood washing himself. He was such a man. She liked to see his neck glistening with water as he swilled it ...

The story evolves in a way characteristic of Lawrence. Firstly, the personalities are in states of intense feeling: sometimes strong emotions conflict within a character. Thus Elsie is described as being simultaneously attracted and repelled by Sam Adams when she dances with him just before her marriage to Whiston. On the one hand she finds the physical closeness and movement of dancing with him hypnotically compelling. On the other hand, part of her remains detached: 'she was not carried away.'

Secondly, these strong emotions are described using repetition of image and idea in order to convey to the reader the waves of powerfully felt but barely understood emotion. As Elsie and Sam dance:

> Every moment, and every moment, she felt she would give way utterly, and sink down molten: the fusion point was coming when she would fuse down into perfect unconsciousness at his feet and knees. But he bore her round the room in the dance, and he seemed to sustain all her body with his limbs, his body, and his warmth seemed to come closer into her, nearer, till it would fuse right through her, and she would be as liquid to him, as an intoxication only.

On a rational level this does not make entirely good sense at a first reading – but the movement of the prose, its rhythm, repetitions and images convey an overwhelmingly strong sense of what was so powerfully felt, but not analytically understood, by the character. In addition, the choice of language in 'bore her', 'all her body', 'his warmth' conveys a seductive sensuality which is entirely appropriate.

Thirdly, any dialogue between characters at highly charged moments seems, as it often does in real life, quite banal, a complete failure of any real communication about the subject which is simultaneously deeply disturbing the participants. Thus when, in an interval between the dancing, the miserably jealous Whiston tackles Elsie about her clear preference for dancing with Sam, their conversation runs as follows:

'I like him,' she said.

'What do you find to like in him?' he said with a hot heart.

'I don't know – but I like him,' she said.

Fourthly, when the tension tips into open conflict between the couple at the end of the story, Elsie, although she feels afraid of her husband's responses, also feels driven to provoke him almost beyond measure whilst not consciously knowing why she is behaving this way:

She was rousing all his uncontrollable anger. He sat glowering. Every one of her sentences stirred him up like a red-hot iron. Soon it would be too much. And she was afraid herself; but she was neither conquered nor convinced.

This is not an unfamiliar dilemma for a female character in Lawrence: she exults in her power to taunt him whilst feeling a real dread of what it is going to lead to. One thinks of Anna's behaviour towards Will in *The Rainbow*.

Fifthly, in the conflict between the characters at the end of the story, Whiston is 'unconscious with a black storm of rage'; he has a 'lust to see her bleed, to break her and destroy her' and is 'moved to kill her' – at least momentarily. However, they come to an anguished reconciliation in the end when she, again typically, submits: 'she let herself be taken.' Conflict in Lawrence is sometimes a way of achieving an understanding, sometimes purely destructive; it is often described in sexual terms. Note the use of the word 'lust' in the quotation above.

Finally, the ending of this story is characteristic of Lawrence. It is open-ended, lacking a sense of solid closure. It ends in inconsequential dialogue – like *Women in Love*. Of course, short stories are less likely to have definitive endings than novels but several of Lawrence's best known novels end not with a bang but a whimper.

'SNAKE'

This well-known poem, written by Lawrence in **free verse**, contains features which are typical of Lawrence's approach both in terms of the ideas and the language in which it is written.

Ideas in the poem

Lawrence presents the material in the first person, although he perhaps expects us to see the persona as a representative of Western civilization rather than being his autobiographical self. He is interested here in the conflict between the strait-jacket of rationality or learned behaviour and the natural, spontaneous and instinctive reaction of the unconscious. You will find this dichotomy elsewhere in Lawrence.

KEYWORD

Free verse: Now a very common form of writing, characterized by a lack of formal structure, a freedom from rigid metrical patterns, and often with no formal rhyming patterns. This does not necessarily imply that that there are no formal devices used in the verse, simply that they do not conform to a traditional pattern – they are often unique to a particular poem.

The poet is living in Sicily. It is the hottest part of the day, 'the intense still noon', in the hottest month, July, and he has walked from the house to the tap over a water-trough to collect water. When he gets there, he sees that a very large snake is just arriving to quench its thirst. The poet's first reaction is to stand humbly aside and wait for the snake to have a drink. Whilst waiting, he observes the reptile closely and admires both the leisurely, graceful movement and the golden-yellow colour of the creature.

However, the poet is not left to his enjoyment for long. The 'voice of my education' intrudes, pointing out that in this part of the world, whilst black snakes are perfectly harmless, 'the gold are venomous'. It goes on to goad him, saying, 'if you were not afraid you would kill him!' The poet is now in a dilemma of his own making. On the one hand, he instinctively feels 'honoured', privileged to watch this beautiful creature which has chosen to visit his trough. On the other hand, a learned response impels him to destroy the very thing which has just been giving him such pleasure. In the end, Lawrence does throw a log at the snake – but in a rather half-hearted way, and at a point at which it is almost too late: the creature has finished drinking and is retreating into the hole from which it had emerged earlier. This does not appear to damage the snake, it only serves to make it disappear 'in undignified haste.'

Lawrence is left bitterly regretting his behaviour, which he now despises as being 'paltry', 'vulgar' and 'mean'. He feels that he was gifted with an opportunity which he has completely failed to live up to: 'I missed my chance with one of the lords of life.'

Language of the poem

The way in which Lawrence uses language in this poem is quite typical of the way in which he works. The third stanza will repay close study and provide useful examples:

> He reached down from a fissure in the earth-wall in the gloom
> And trailed his yellow-brown **s**lackness **s**oft-bellied down, over the edge
>   of the **s**tone trough
> And rested his throat upon the **s**tone bottom,
> And where the water had dripped from the tap, in a **s**mall clearne**ss**,
> He **s**ipped with his **s**traight mouth,
> **S**oftly drank through his **s**traight gums, into his **s**lack long body,
> **S**ilently.

Lawrence uses the repeated **s** sound (emboldened above) and long vowel sounds – as in 'reached', 'trailed' – to suggest the languorous, sliding movement of the snake. He uses repetition for the same reason, both with key words like soft/softly to suggest the potential vulnerability of the creature, and with the repeated, leisurely 'and' at the beginnings of lines. Apart from the last 'silently', the lines here are also protracted. This is very different from the abrupt, jerky movement of a later stanza which also contains much sharper sounds:

> I looked round, I put down my pitcher,
> I picked up a clumsy log
> And threw it at the water-trough with a clatter.

Lawrence uses repeated words which suggest golden light or the opposite, a sinister black, in this poem to build and convey the polarity of his ideas. Both are associated with the snake, appropriately, because it is both compellingly beautiful and deadly. It is thus 'earth-golden' whilst having a 'tongue like a forked night on the air, so black' and it disappears into 'the dark door of the secret earth.' There is something decidedly repellent about its 'withdrawing into that horrid black hole'; this not only suggests a creature of the underworld but has decided phallic overtones.

Finally, Lawrence uses allusion to convey his ideas in this poem as he so often does elsewhere in his writing. At the end of the poem, full of shame for his 'pettiness', Lawrence thinks of 'the albatross' – and the reader immediately remembers Coleridge's poem 'The Ancient Mariner' and its message of suffering and expiated guilt.

✳ ✳ ✳*SUMMARY*✳ ✳ ✳

Prose is characterized by:

- characters who are in states of great intensity of feeling

- emotions which are described using repetition

- seemingly banal dialogue

- female characters who are driven to taunt their partners

- conflict which can become violent and which is described in sexual terms

- no solid closure at end.

Poetry and prose are characterized by:

- use of sound and vivid image

- interest in polarity of ideas

- use of allusion.

3 Biography and influences

Lawrence is a writer whose life is inextricably woven with his work. Not only were certain people – his mother, his first girlfriend, Miriam, his wife, Frieda – an overwhelming influence, but Lawrence was a writer who used his own experiences more productively than most in his writing. He had a magpie mind which seized upon and used – almost, one might say, shamelessly – any experiences or people he encountered. As a consequence, he had to deal with threatened libel cases such as that by Philip Heseltine who saw that Halliday and Pussum from *Women in Love* were derived from himself and his wife. He also had to cope with

several abrupt endings to friendships when those close to him recognized an unflattering portrait of themselves in his writing. Lady Ottoline Morrell felt appalled and betrayed by Lady Hermione Roddice in *The Rainbow*. Lawrence had used certain aspects of her personality in this fictional character which created, she felt, a caricature of herself. She was another who threatened to sue and who immediately ceased contact with Lawrence. The Meynells never allowed the author's name to be mentioned in their hearing again after the unforgivable abuse of their hospitality represented by the publication of Lawrence's story 'England, My England'. This does not mean that characters or events are unambiguously replicated from life; it does mean that a sound understanding of Lawrence's life is most helpful in appreciating his work.

LAWRENCE'S FAMILY

Lawrence's mother was undoubtedly the formative influence in his life. Born Lydia Beardsall, she was from a genteel family with intellectual aspirations which had fallen on hard times. When she first met Arthur Lawrence, a miner, she was smarting from the recent preference shown by her intended for a wealthy widow. Just as described in *Sons and Lovers* she was smitten by Arthur's liberating sense of fun and capacity for getting the most out of life. However, once married, like the Morels and for the same reasons, their happiness did not last. Feeling trapped and increasingly embittered, Mrs Lawrence made certain that her three sons (of whom Lawrence was the youngest) and two daughters inherited both her tenacious educational aspirations (she was going to ensure that none of her sons ever went down the pit) and the contempt she increasingly felt for her husband. It would take Lawrence years to escape both from his mother's stifling love and the dislike she instilled in him of his own father. He only began to take a more balanced view of his father's undoubted good qualities – and to regret the picture he had painted of him in *Sons and Lovers* – very much later on.

As a child, Lawrence was very close to his mother. However, the son she idolized was her eldest, William Ernest. Both the eldest and youngest sons won scholarships to Nottingham High School and did well there. William Ernest seemed set on a brilliant course for a successful future in London when he became ill and died at the age of 23. His mother was plunged into apathy and depression by his death and she was roused out of this only by her youngest son falling dangerously ill with pneumonia. In her unremitting fight to save Lawrence from a tragic, premature end, she poured all her emotional energy into the relationship and bound him to her with a passion from which he only escaped by her death nine years later.

Lawrence's greatest debt to his mother – apart from the material for *Sons and Lovers* – was probably the ability she gave him of understanding the female psyche. Feminist critics have found much to complain of in some of Lawrence's writing, but most would agree that he is intuitively close to the minds and feelings of his female characters in a way he sometimes fails to be with regard to his male characters.

Jessie Chambers was the second crucial female influence on Lawrence's life; she encouraged him in all his early writing. Miriam in *Sons and Lovers* is based on Jessie – although like many people subsequently, she was not pleased with her portrait there, feeling it undervalued the quality of their intellectual interaction. His visits to Haggs Farm gave Lawrence the opportunity to enjoy the kind of healthy, honest physical labour from which he derived satisfaction.

Lawrence and Jessie shared a great deal of reading and lively discussion. They became pupil teachers; Lawrence passed the King's Scholarship examination which gave him a free place at a teacher training college and he coached Jessie to achieve the same success. However, after years of friendship the relationship finally began to peter out.

MEN IN LAWRENCE'S LIFE

Jessie's eldest brother, Alan, was also an important influence. Lawrence was no closet homosexual; indeed he had a deep fear of 'men loving men' as he explained in a letter to David Garnett in 1915. He found the whole idea quite repellent. However, as a young man he clearly felt some sort of admiring physical attraction as well as straightforward friendship for Alan and this is mirrored in *The White Peacock*, where, by his own admission, the handsome, virile hero, George, is based on him. At one point George and the narrator, Cyril, swim naked in a mill-pond on a fine June morning, and then George towels Cyril dry. The description is notably sensuous and clearly influenced by the affection Lawrence felt for Alan.

Later on, other men were also an influence and clearly helped Lawrence to feel, like Birkin in *Women in Love*, that he would ideally like a satisfying, although not necessarily physical, relationship with another man. Lawrence felt attracted to John Middleton Murry and Birkin in *Women in Love* may be partially based on him, although this is a character who also has a good deal in common with Lawrence himself. In that novel, Birkin struggles with unwelcome but undeniable feelings of desire for Gerald Crich – another character who owed a debt to a real man – who was probably based, in part, on William Henry Hocking, a neighbour of the Lawrences in Cornwall. Some biographers of Lawrence have concluded that it is likely that this particular friendship came to fruition in an expression of physical love between the two men in the summer of 1917.

FRIEDA WEEKLEY

Lawrence took up his first teaching post in Croydon in 1908. There followed four frustrating years during which he desperately wanted to find a satisfying physical relationship with a woman but failed to achieve one. His health was precarious and he still suffered from his mother's death which had occurred at the end of 1910; however, as a writer he was becoming increasingly recognized. In March 1912, he met Frieda Weekley which at least addressed the sexual problem fairly immediately. Frieda was five years older than Lawrence, a German aristocrat and a lady with a colourful sexual past. She was also the wife of a professor of modern languages at Nottingham University College and the mother of his three children. Less than two months after their first meeting, Frieda abandoned her husband and children and left England with Lawrence. They married once Frieda's divorce had come through in 1914. Together the couple travelled across Europe and later to Ceylon, Australia, the USA and New Mexico, never staying in one house for any great length of time. They were journeying partly in search of a better climate for Lawrence's health and partly out of sheer restlessness.

THE WAR OF MARRIAGE

The kind of relationship Lawrence had with his wife had a huge impact both on him and his writing. Life with Frieda was inspirational, tempestuous and in some ways rather schizophrenic: Lawrence needed her and loved her passionately – but she irritated him beyond endurance and he occasionally came near to murdering her. The balance of power between the two never settled at an easy, mutually acceptable equilibrium: one thing which life with Frieda confirmed in Lawrence's mind was that a male/female relationship necessarily involved endless struggle and fight. A procession of visitors to the Lawrences recorded the rather startling aggressive violence which the couple could display, regardless of on-lookers, a violence which was often immediately followed, even more surprisingly, by quiet domestic chat. Nevertheless, despite how things may have at times appeared, the couple chose on the whole to stay together and Lawrence clearly missed Frieda when they were apart. Moreover, despite the lack of absolute perfection in his own marriage, Lawrence continued throughout his life to affirm his belief in the central importance of a solid union between man and wife.

Lawrence had to put up with Frieda's infidelities, sometimes conducted fairly blatantly under his nose. She had to endure his lack of understanding over her utter misery at the loss of her children, the eldest of whom was only twelve when she left England with Lawrence. They both had to face up to the disappointment of gradually realizing that they would not have children of their own.

However, critics have recognized that whereas in earlier novels, both men and women seem equally at fault in the failure of relationships, there is a shift in such later stories as 'The Woman Who Rode Away' and 'St Mawr' - and this may have stemmed from the changing relationship between Lawrence and his wife. In these stories, independent women seem something of a threat and are made to suffer. Lawrence, who was growing increasingly unwell, was also increasingly angry and bitter. By the time he revised *Lady Chatterley's Lover* for the third time at the end of 1927, there was perhaps an element of himself in the impotent Clifford Chatterley – and there must have been a frisson of frustration, or perhaps just wish-fulfilment, behind his depiction of the sex which he was aware that Frieda was enjoying with her new lover, Angelo Ravagli.

Lawrence had only three more years to live. He finally succumbed to the tuberculosis which both he and Frieda had long endeavoured to pretend did not exist, in 1930.

✹ ✹ ✹ *SUMMARY* ✹ ✹ ✹

● Lawrence draws heavily on his own experience in his writing.

● He was strongly influenced by his mother and the relationship he had with her.

● Lawrence's longing for a rewarding, non-sexual relationship with another man was an important factor in his attitude to relationships.

● His tempestuous marriage with Frieda influenced his attitude to sexual partnerships.

4 Major works – four key novels

We are going to sample four major novels which span Lawrence's most creative period: *Sons and Lovers, The Rainbow, Women in Love* and *Lady Chatterley's Lover.* In each of these novels, characters struggle to deal with various constraints which hamper their forming satisfying relationships.

After a brief glance at the individual characteristics of these novels, we will touch on the psychological accuracy with which Lawrence develops relationships and the style of his writing which clarifies central ideas for the reader.

SONS AND LOVERS

Sons and Lovers was Lawrence's third novel and, like Dickens's *David Copperfield*, it solidly establishes a background into which a hero is born, grows up and develops through experiences like acquiring his first job and girlfriend. So far, so conventional. You may find it referred to as a **Könstlerroman**, which is a version of the **Bildungsroman**.

Lawrence undoubtedly used his own experience very fully in this novel. Lawrence's parents' relationship, attitudes and

personalities are mirrored in that of the Morels. His own experiences as a child, including his dread of having to go and collect his father's pay packet from the colliery offices, provide material here and lend the stamp of authenticity to such scenes as that in which Walter gets his children to help him make fuses for use in the mine. His emotional involvement with his mother, and the way in which that relationship impinged on that with his first girlfriend, Jessie Chambers, is followed in the Paul/Miriam relationship. Even the death of Mrs Morel – from the cancer which killed Lawrence's own mother – and Lawrence's subsequent feelings of suicidal depression are used in the novel.

By the time Lawrence was revising *Sons and Lovers* he was living with Frieda Weekly. Some critics, quoting Lawrence's remark in a letter to A. W. McLeod in 1913 that 'one sheds one's sickness in books', choose to see *Sons and Lovers* as a way of his coming to terms with those formative experiences which had made him the man he was. However, it is probably unhelpful and misleading to side with early critics and regard the novel as straightforwardly autobiographical: Lawrence's experiences are clearly fictionalized. In any case, Lawrence, who can usually be relied on to contradict himself, made an earlier statement in a letter to Sydney Pawling that the novel on which he was currently working was 'restrained, somewhat impersonal.'

THE RAINBOW AND WOMEN IN LOVE

These two novels can, in one way, be seen as presenting one body of material – because that is how they began life. Lawrence re-worked his material several times as usual – no less than eight in this case. It was first called *The Sisters* then *Wedding Ring* before being split and re-drafted as *The Rainbow* and *Women in Love*. In some senses the latter is a continuation of the former: they have themes and characters in common. Lawrence himself wrote in a letter that '*The Rainbow* and *Women in Love* are really an organic artistic whole.'

However, there are very great differences between the two. Firstly, and very obviously, the reader soon notices that the time-spans of the two are completely dissimilar. *The Rainbow* is a great sweeping panorama of a novel covering several decades; even the opening sentence suggests this leisurely approach:

> The Brangwens had lived for generations on the Marsh Farm, in the meadows where the Erewash twisted sluggishly through alder trees, separating Derbyshire from Nottinghamshire.

The novel presents a strong sense of ever-widening concentric circles to the reader – both Chapters 10 and 14 are entitled 'The Widening Circle'. This is inevitably created in part by dealing with successive generations of the Brangwen family – but it is also because of the period of change during which they live. Marsh Farm, the unchanging solid centre of the novel, is 'just on the safe side of civilisation.' Here, Tom Brangwen is born, from here he courts Lydia Lensky and marries her, his children are born here, and here he finally dies. His step-daughter, Anna, spends her childhood, and then much of her married life in the local village, only later moving to the more industrialized town of Beldover when her oldest daughter, Ursula, is 17. Ursula first attends the village school in Cossethay, then moves to the High School in the city of Nottingham before earning her independent living as a teacher and going to college.

Women in Love, on the other hand, covers barely one year in the lives of the characters. In the opening chapter, Ursula and her younger sister, Gudrun, discuss their attitudes to marriage in a sisterly scene which verges on the conventional. Thereafter, however, their search for meaning in life and relationships takes them through a densely written, closely connected series of scenes which brings them into contact with different aspects of modern society and moves them across Europe.

Secondly, there is a difference in tone. Lawrence's vision is decidedly bleaker in *Women in Love*, something he recognized himself when he wrote in a letter that this second novel was 'purely destructive, not like *The Rainbow*, destructive-consummating.' Various disappointments and difficulties had embittered him to an extent: the banning of *The Rainbow*; problems with private friendships; his struggle with Frieda and their difficulties surviving in England during the First World War.

A stratum deeper

It is worth appreciating that Lawrence was consciously intending something new and different when he wrote these novels. His ideas are usefully set out for us in a series of letters written to Edward Garnett during 1913 and 1914. Lawrence felt the need to explain that he was consciously moving away from his previous style: 'I have no longer the joy in creating vivid scenes, that I had in *Sons and Lovers*'. In the same letter, he points out, 'I have a different attitude to characters' and consequently 'that necessitates a different attitude in you.' He goes on to explain, 'that which is psychic – non-human, in humanity, is more interesting to me than the old-fashioned human element – which causes one to conceive a character in a certain moral scheme and make him consistent … You mustn't look in my novel for the old stable **ego** of the character.'

This, in practice, does not mean that characters are inconsistent or unbelievable, despite what early critics may have had to say, (see Contemporary Critical Approaches p. 57–8). The character of Ursula Brangwen, for instance, does not fluctuate between the different chapters in *Women in Love*; she presents the same coherent personality there as she does in *The Rainbow*. However, it is clear that she does not move through an elaborately plotted series of circumstances, particularly in *Women in Love*. What interests Lawrence is this person as a type of humanity both instinctively and rationally dealing with the question which engages every character in the novels and, one could argue, in life: How can I become myself and be fulfilled in the best possible way? Ursula, as a young girl, actually asks, 'Wither to go, how to become oneself?'

LADY CHATTERLEY'S LOVER

Lady Chatterley's Lover is probably the most widely known of Lawrence's novels. This is, unfortunately, because of the furore which accompanied its initial publication rather than because of its undoubted literary strengths. Lawrence knew he would have difficulty with publication; hence he arranged to have the novel first published privately in Florence in 1928. It was banned in England for 32 years after that, achieving massive circulation immediately after the acquittal of Penguin Books in an obscenity trial at the end of 1960.

There are two significant ironies inherent in the initial notoriety of *Lady Chatterley's Lover*. One is that the banning of the book by the English authorities ensured exactly the sort of prurient interest in the book which Lawrence deplored. One of his aims in writing it had been to get people to see sex – and the four-letter words associated with it – as something natural and beautiful, life-giving in every sense. In *A Propos of Lady Chatterley's Lover* he wrote: 'I want men and women to be able to *think* sex, fully, complete, honestly, and cleanly.' The result of the ban, however, was that imported copies were passed round in plain brown paper covers to the accompaniment of much furtive, salacious interest and embarrassed tittering.

Another irony is that the book was the first to be prosecuted under the Obscene Publications Act of 1959: this was originally drawn up with a view to protecting works of real literary merit which happened to include sexual detail – like *Lady Chatterley's Lover* – from squalid pornographic material it was felt needed to be restricted.

Several decades later, and in a very different moral climate, the novel can now be more readily appreciated for its acutely perceptive observations of interactions between people – interactions not always involving sex. A novel explicitly detailing the pleasures of sex between a man and a woman of different social classes – where it is the woman who belongs to the higher social orders – no longer shocks.

PSYCHOLOGICAL ACCURACY

Lawrence is particularly good at describing how, when relationships are shaky, any given situation can quickly take a downward spiral almost before the participants realize what is happening. An example of this occurs in *Sons and Lovers* a few years into the Morels' marriage. Walter Morel decides to spend a day walking with a friend. Mrs Morel feels indignant on several counts: she can't stand the friend; she knows the day's activity will involve Morel in drinking; this leaves her, heavily pregnant, to cope on a hot day on her own with two small children. When Morel returns in the evening, he too is feeling out of sorts – although perhaps with less justification than his wife. He has fallen asleep in the hot sun and drinking both before and after this nap have not improved his temper – although 'he did not know he was angry.' He also has 'a bad conscience', which doesn't help. When he comes into the kitchen, his wife is making home-made beer – just the sort of task to be a particular irritant on this occasion. He sways slightly and lurches against the table, which causes her rather self-righteous remark, 'Good gracious, coming home in this drunkenness!' This serves to unleash a degree of temper in Morel which he barely knew he possessed.

NARRATIVE VIEWPOINT

Lawrence's narrative viewpoint can help us to see events from the standpoint of several characters. *Sons and Lovers* is an example of this subtly shifting narrative viewpoint. Although events are presented from Paul's point of view, Lawrence allows us to see and sympathize with Miriam's standpoint. On the one hand Paul tells us that Miriam is immature, clinging, possessive and frigid. On the other hand, the reader can see that at least she doesn't indulge in repetitive infantile fantasies of going off and living with her mother in a county cottage somewhere like Paul does – and she does choose to give herself freely to Paul in what appears, in the context of the time, a fairly daring move. Because Paul is himself confused and prone to self-deception, he is not the most reliable of narrators. There is, too, a sense in which the characters are not in control of themselves: Paul says to Miriam, 'But you are what your unconscious self makes you, not so much what you want to be.'

Similarly, although we are invited to side with Mrs Morel against her husband, it is possible to see Mrs Morel as a really rather difficult woman whilst he is an attractive figure in many ways. One thinks of her only response to her husband's bringing her a cup of tea in bed in the morning being (*a*) she didn't want it anyway and (*b*) he has almost certainly forgotten to add the sugar.

SYMBOLISM

Sometimes Lawrence plays out a scene in which one person or a pair of characters respond very differently to some natural phenomenon. These are intensely memorable episodes which project potent ideas about the interplay of personalities, ideas which are impossible to convey adequately in a conventional novel. A selection of examples from the four novels is mentioned below.

The moon

There are four crucial scenes in *The Rainbow* where women confront the moon with three different men. Anna Lensky and later her daughter Ursula enjoy exposing themselves to the brilliant moonlight, whereas Will Brangwen and Anton Skrebensky shrink away. The two women can be seen as dominant in their responses – these are not couples in an even balance with each other. Ursula finally destroys Skrebensky in a moonlit scene on the dunes. Although each successive moonlit scene is incredibly powerful, it is not immediately obvious what the moon 'means'. Nicholas Marsh, in his *D. H. Lawrence: The Novels* (St Martin's Press, 2000) suggests that although 'the moon stands for hard self-will and withdrawal from relationships', it is not quite as simple as that; Lawrence is creating a multi-layered effect by many associations and metaphors which all contribute to the depth of the symbol. Marsh's chapter is well worth reading.

It pays to look further. *Women in Love* provides the interesting chapter called 'Moony' in which Birkin throws stones at the reflection of the moon in water. Meanwhile, *Sons and Lovers* includes one early scene in which Mrs Morel is in her garden after a late evening contretemps with her husband and a further one when Paul and Miriam walk along a moonlit beach whilst on holiday. Their different responses to the moon in this episode highlight their very different feelings. For reference to Helen Baron's analysis of the first of these two episodes see p. 74 in the chapter in 'Disseminated Consciousness in *Sons and Lovers*', Essays in Critisism (Oct, 1998), 'Modern Critical Approaches'.

Gerald and the arab mare

Another typical example of Lawrence's use of symbolism to give information about character, theme and relationships is his treatment of the episode in which Gerald masters his horse, forcing her to stand at the level crossing gates despite her terror, whilst a colliery train passes. This develops over some four-and-a-half pages at the beginning of the chapter entitled 'Coal-dust' in *Women in Love*. As so often in Lawrence, the summary of the event sounds ridiculously banal, the kind of thing which might have been dismissed briskly in one or at most two sentences by another author. Lawrence's method conveys meaning both powerfully and unforgettably.

Lawrence uses words with hard consonant sounds here to underscore the train's unnatural, loud mechanical noise which so terrifies the horse: '… back came the trucks rebounding on the iron buffers, striking like cymbals, clashing nearer and nearer in frightful strident concussions.' The mare's reaction to this is stressed by the use of figurative language which suggests the opposition of the natural and the man-made: '… the mare rebounded like a drop of water from hot iron.' A telling feature of this episode is that Ursula and Gudrun, who are watching, have exactly the same response as the mare, they 'pressed back into the hedge, in fear.'

Gerald is described as delighting both in mastering the animal and in inflicting pain on her. He appears to be revelling in the experience, his face is 'shining with fixed amusement', and, rather chillingly, especially in view of his end, is 'calm as a ray of cold sunshine.' Lawrence also implies, through the language used, that this is a man who enjoys brutal sexual domination. Initially, Gerald is described as riding 'well and softly, pleased with the delicate quivering of the creature between his knees.' Once he has engaged in struggling with the animal's will:

> … he held on her unrelaxed, with an almost mechanical relentlessness, keen as a sword pressing into her. Both man and horse were sweating with violence.

Although Ursula and Gudrun have initially responded in the same way to the train, they have very different reactions to Gerald's behaviour. Ursula is 'frantic with opposition and hatred of Gerald.' She continues to feel quite implacably revulsed. However, Gudrun, who has felt 'quite hard and cold and indifferent' when watching, can't get the image out of her head. When she remembers it, she herself sees it, fascinatedly, in sexual terms:

> Gudrun was as if numbed in her mind by the sense of the man, bearing down into the living body of the horse: the strong indomitable thighs of the blond man clenching the palpitating body of the mare into pure control; a sort of soft white magnetic domination from the loins and thighs and calves, enclosing and encompassing the mare heavily into unutterable subordination.'

Although part of her responds to this as being 'terrible', another part thrills to it.

After reading this episode we have a strong understanding of the sado-masochistic nature of the attraction which will develop between Gerald and Gudrun. It also serves to ally Gerald, the mine-owner's son, with the relentless, inhumane advance of the mining industry. Just as he masters the natural fear of the horse without any consideration for its independent spirit or finer feelings, so mine-owners like him will insist on the encroachment of the countryside and the mechanization of the mines without any appreciation for what they are destroying.

The rainbow

An important symbol used in *The Rainbow* is the rainbow of the title, together with allied images of arches and doorways. Thus, when things are not going well between Lydia and Tom, he feels 'like a broken arch thrust sickeningly out for support.' For a time, Tom tries to find 'another centre of love in her child, Anna.' Once Tom establishes his relationship with Lydia he is not needy of the child any more; she is free to be herself within the solid, happy atmosphere prevailing in her home. This is memorably described:

Anna's soul was put at peace between them. She looked from one to the other, and she saw them established to her safety and she was free ... She was no longer called upon to uphold with her childish might the broken end of the arch. Her mother and her father now met in the span of the heavens, and she, the child, was free to play in the space beneath.'

Lawrence uses this symbol throughout the novel in a relatively conventional way to suggest the promise of spiritual fulfilment which characters might attain, usually together, through a relationship. He combines this with allusion from and rhythmic echoes of the Authorized Version of the Bible to convey forceful ideas about relationships to the reader.

✳ ✳ ✳ SUMMARY ✳ ✳ ✳

- *Sons and Lovers* is based on Lawrence's early life.

- *The Rainbow* and *Woman in Love* share some characters and themes, although in other ways they are different.

- Lawrence aimed to make sexual words and descriptions more natural in *Lady Chatterley's Lover*.

- Both psychological accuracy and a shifting narrative viewpoint help the reader to a subtle appreciation of these novels.

- Style, particularly symbolism and image, help us to understand the interactions between characters.

Major works – poetry

Penguin's edition of *Complete Poems*, (ed. Pinto and Roberts, 1994) is a good place to access Lawrence's poetry. Much of it is written in free verse and has the quality of spontaneous thought or speech. Some, however, has a disciplined rhyming scheme, including several written with the rhythms of colloquial speech and dialect; these have a moving simplicity and directness. Lawrence shows considerable skill in deploying rhythm and sound effects in poetry; he is also a master of vivid visual detail. Take, for example, the dramatic image which arrests our attention at the opening of 'Wedding Morn':

> The morning breaks like a pomegranate
> In a shining crack of red

WIT AND SARCASM

Sometimes Lawrence uses humour to make a serious point, as in 'Wages' or 'A Sane Revolution'. In other poems, like 'Red Geranium and Godly Mignonette', his sense of the ridiculous surfaces when he considers the creation of these flowers in conventional biblical terms. Before dismissing the thought, he toys with the idea of 'the Most High' as divine conjuror, who might have been straining his mighty mind

> to think, among the moss and mud of lizards and mastodons
> to think out, in the abstract, when all was twilit green and muddy:
> 'Now there shall be tum-tiddly-um, and tum-tiddly-um,
> hey-presto! scarlet geranium!'

In 'Peach', Lawrence neatly opens and closes his poem with the tongue-in-cheek idea that the listener could well find his meanderings on peaches so irritating that he might like to avail himself of the remains of Lawrence's peach, the stone, to throw at the poet. The body of the poem contains the most successfully sensuous description of the fruit

– 'voluptuous heavy' with its 'lovely bivalve roundness' and 'silvery peach-bloom' – so much more attractive than any man-made item.

THE NATURAL WORLD

Lawrence delighted in the natural world and conveyed his sensitive, tender appreciation of it most vividly in his poetry. He had a kind of reverence for creatures which means that his portraits of them are never mawkish, sentimental or anthropomorphic. 'Mountain Lion' is a good example of this kind of poem. Here Lawrence recounts how, when 'climbing through January snow, into the Lobo canyon' up a difficult trail, he encountered two men. His first reaction is apprehension, on principle, because men are 'the only animal in the world to fear' – a feeling accentuated by the realization that they have a gun whereas he does not. He sees that one of the men is carrying something which he takes first for a deer before recognizing it as a mountain lion which they have trapped. The next stanza is a poignant hymn of praise to the beauty of the dead creature with her beautifully marked 'round, bright face, bright as frost.'

The poet continues up the trail and comes across the dead animal's lair where she was until recently, at one with her environment, part of the stunningly beautiful surroundings. Lawrence ends the poem with a reflection that whilst the world could easily 'spare a million or two of humans / And never miss them', the death of this mountain lion creates a terrible 'gap.' One is reminded in this poem of 'Snake' (see Chapter 2, page 8–10) and the sense there of the grace and beauty of the reptile in its natural surroundings; this is something that man has no right to interfere with.

There are many other poems about the natural world to enjoy. In 'Bat', the cadence of the verse reflects the movement of the creature:

> A circle swoop, and a quick parabola under the bridge arches
> Where light pushes through …

'Humming-Bird' captures movement too; here Lawrence imagines that at the beginning of creation:

> This little bit chipped off in brilliance
> And went whizzing through the slow, vast, succulent stems.

This is a poem with rather a surprise ending. You might also like to look at the sequence of poems on tortoises – the babies are described as 'little perambulating pebbles' in 'Tortoise Family Connections'.

POEMS OF THOUGHT AND FEELING

Lawrence's childhood

A study of Lawrence's poetry of personal thought allows the reader a window into experiences with which it is easy to empathize. In 'Discord in Childhood', he recalls himself as a child listening to a storm raging in the world outside the house. As the wind rises, 'the lash of the tree / Shrieked and slashed the wind.' This same imagery of a violent destructive force is continued in the second stanza when he describes what he is hearing in the house. The frightened child hears two angry voices, 'a slender lash' and a more dominant 'thick lash booming and bruising.' Meanwhile, outside, the wild crashing discords of the tree echo those inside.

This is one of several poems where the same material was also used in *Sons and Lovers*. In the novel, Paul Morel, huddled upstairs in bed, hears 'the booming shouts of his father, come home drunk, then the sharp replies of his mother … then the whole was drowned in a piercing medley of shrieks and cries from the great, windswept ash-tree.' 'Cherry Robbers' and 'Sorrow' are two other poems, the contents of which are interestingly echoed in events in the novel.

LAWRENCE'S EXPERIENCE WITH FRIEDA

The sequence of poems entitled *Look! We Have Come Through* are particularly personal. These poems form a record of his early relationship with Frieda Weekley from early adrenalin surge through discomforting struggle to mutual acceptance.

One striking poem from this collection is called 'Gloire de Dijon', the name of a particular type of rose, a deliciously scented old variety with the palest apricot-cream head of thick crumpled petals. We are invited to see a woman through the eyes of a satisfied lover who chooses to 'linger' in their bed for the sake of the sheer enjoyment of continuing to watch her as she washes:

> … down her sides the mellow
> Golden shadow glows as
> She stoops to the sponge, and her swung breasts
> Sway like full-blown yellow
> Gloire de Dijon roses.

The poem is redolent with contentment, satiety and, appropriately, golden sunlight and silken skin/roses. The woman's leisurely, rhythmic movements, 'stoops to the sponge', 'swung breasts / Sway' is reflected in the soft, easy **alliteration** and in the movement of the verse.

KEYWORD

Alliteration: repetition of the same sounds, usually the initial consonants of words, or stressed syllables in neighbouring words, for special effect, e.g. the murmuring of innumerable bees.

THOUGHTS ABOUT LIFE AND DEATH

At the very end of his life, Lawrence wrote several poems about death. 'Bavarian Gentians' and 'The Ship of Death' are powerful and compelling. Another poem written at this time, 'Poverty', is a reflection on his life: he points out that having experienced real hardship in his life, he has no wish to be poor – but neither does he long for riches. He uses the inspiration of a tree, a symbol recurrent in literature to stand for something firmly rooted in solid actuality whilst growing towards the spirituality of the sky and combines this with allusion to the Christian symbols of Christ's body and blood:

With its roots it has a grand grip on its daily bread,
and its plumes look like green cups held up to sun and air and full of wine.
I want to be like that, to have a natural abundance
and plume forth, and be splendid.

This pine-tree, despite its unpromising situation on a rocky cliff-face, is flourishing despite everything and is reaching outward and upward joyously – celebrating and enjoying the moment, as D. H. Lawrence did.

✳ ✳ ✳ *SUMMARY* ✳ ✳ ✳

- There is enormous variety in Lawrence's poetry – both in terms of style and subject matter.

- Some poems deploy wit to amuse or drive home a serious point.

- His best poems about the natural world are crisply and vividly compelling.

- Lawrence's poems of thought and feeling spring directly from his own experience and sometimes echo ideas in his novels.

---

6 Major themes

One important thing to notice about Lawrence's writing is that it is built around the central concept of what some critics have called polarity, others duality. This is the theory that opposites not only attract, they also repel and in so doing are balanced and held firmly together. You might find it easier to think of this in terms of the eastern concept of the yin and the yang. Thus, every individual, whether male or female, has both masculine and feminine characteristics held in balance. When individuals enter into a relationship, they need to find the right complementary balance between themselves – and as far as Lawrence is concerned this will inevitably involve conflict.

FINDING A BALANCE THROUGH CONFLICT: CONSTRUCTIVE RELATIONSHIPS

Lawrence believed in the salvation of the individual through a healthy sexual relationship; this is a central theme. For him a healthy relationship involved simultaneous climax. He also believed in the cleansing effect which anal intercourse could have within the context of a well-balanced relationship. He saw success in relationships as only achieved after enormous struggle. One has only to look at the titles of individual poems in *Look We Have Come Through*, Lawrence's volume about his honeymoon with Frieda, to see this. There is one entitled 'Elysium' but there is also 'Loggerheads' and 'Why Does She Weep?' In *Phoenix 11: Unpublished and Other Prose Works by D. H. Lawrence* (ed. Warren Roberts and Harry T. Moore, Heinemann, 1968) we find him declaring that 'in people of strong, individual feeling, the irritation that accumulates in marriage increases only too often to a point of rage that is akin to madness.' This might not be everyone's experience, but it was clearly Lawrence's, and it affected the way he thought and wrote.

One way to look at Lawrence's ideas is to look closely at how he depicts successful relationships. And there aren't many of these. Arguably, the most successful is that between Tom Brangwen and Lydia Lensky in *The Rainbow*: this couple experience one significant glitch early on – but then their very successful marriage lasts 25 years until Tom's death. The relationship between Mellors and Connie in *Lady Chatterley's Lover* works very well; they are waiting to be in a position to marry at the end of the novel. However, common sense indicates that although all the signs for their future happiness augur well, they have not yet had any real day-to-day experience of living together. The marriage of Ursula Brangwen and Rupert Birkin in *Women in Love* appears very successful – but they have been together only for a very short time and Birkin appears to feel restive about wanting a satisfying relationship with a man as well as that with Ursula in order to make him completely content. Critics have divided on whether this is a relationship which will continue to blossom and it remains for the reader to decide.

SUCCESSFUL RELATIONSHIPS

Tom and Lydia

As a young man, Tom in *The Rainbow* thinks that 'he wanted to marry, to get settled somehow', but the right woman fails to present herself. He feels dissatisfied and incomplete: the only partial solution is to go in for bouts of brandy drinking. By this method he achieves a 'kindled state of oneness with all the world.' However, Tom recognizes that this is a less than satisfactory way of conducting his life and Lawrence indicates this to us very clearly:

> 'But he had achieved his satisfaction by obliterating his own individuality, that which it depended on his manhood to preserve and develop.'

At the age of 28, Tom passes Lydia, a newcomer to the district, in a lane. His response is immediate, instinctive and quite decided: 'That's her,' he said involuntarily. Since Lydia is Polish and her English is not entirely fluent, there are initial minor misunderstandings due to differences in culture and language. Communication is at an instinctive rather than a verbal level. Even after their marriage, the feeling between the two fluctuates between glorious, ecstatic fulfilment and acutely frustrating periods when Lydia chooses to distance herself from Tom. The latter infuriate him: '… he lay still and wide-eyed with rage, inarticulate, not understanding, but solid with hostility'. However, a crucial ingredient in the eventual success of their relationship is that Tom recognizes 'he had to learn to contain himself' even when he feels bitterly resentful and hurt by her apparent coldness and selfishness. Thus, although 'he raged, and piled up accusations that had some measure of truth in them all … a certain grace in him forbade him from going too far.' He might want to 'smash her into regarding him. He had a raging agony of desire to do so.' But because 'he did not want to lose her' he makes himself leave her alone. This is a critically important thing for him to learn.

Lawrence expects couples to come into conflict and feel hatred and/or quite violent anger for each other. It is how they deal with these quite inevitable emotions that matters. He felt it was essential for each individual in a couple to remain as strong, separate individuals, to respect each other as such and to achieve a balance of understanding with each other.

After a crisis two years into their marriage Tom and Lydia reach a mutual understanding and their lives come together in 'a sort of richness, a deep inarticulate interchange which made other places seem thin and unsatisfying.' Tom comes to regard 'the long marital embrace' with his wife as by far the best thing in it; it is 'eternal'. After his death, she knows that he 'had made himself immortal in his knowledge with her.'

Ursula and Birkin

Like Ursula's grandfather, Tom Brangwen, at a similar age, Birkin feels restless, incomplete and ready for what he sees as the 'panacea' of marriage at the beginning of *Women in Love*. However, he is a much more educated man and has thought and reasoned a great deal on the subject of what exactly it is that he wants from a relationship. He wants the 'binding contract' of marriage but he does not want 'the old way of love' because 'the thought of love, marriage and children and a life lived together in the terrible privacy of domestic and connubial satisfaction was repulsive.' He is not interested in a settled existence surrounded by possessions; like Lawrence himself, he gives up his job to travel abroad indefinitely with Ursula. This idea of leading a life untrammelled by material possessions is also dealt with in the poem 'New Houses, New Clothes'. Both Birkin and Ursula see clearly that they need to go further than 'love' to achieve something timeless; they strive towards the sense of the beyond, the timeless and eternal which Tom and Lydia achieved. Like Tom and Lydia, they see their relationship as something which will transcend death. Birkin says:

> 'If I die, you'll know I haven't left you.'
> 'And me?' she cried.
> 'And you won't have left me,' he said. 'We shan't have any need to despair, in death.'

Birkin talks of an ideal 'strange conjunction' with Ursula, 'an equilibrium, a pure balance of two single beings: 'as the stars balance each other.' They will remain two completely separate individuals who will complement each other. Although this is clearly Lawrence's ideal, critics have pointed out, often quoting Lawrence's own advice to 'Never trust the artist. Trust the tale' from *Studies in Classic American Literature,* that although Birkin *says* this, his actions do not wholly support his words. Kate Millett, in *Sexual Politics* (Virago, 1981), was one of the first critics to observe that despite his wordy posturing, what Birkin really appears to want is complete dominance of Ursula. She supports this point by quoting the passage from the chapter entitled 'Mino' where Birkin comments approvingly on the male cat's bullying attitude to the female and her acceptance of it.

In addition, Birkin feels that, in an ideal world, he needs something else as well. He explains to Ursula that:

> Having you, I can live all my life without anybody else, any other sheer intimacy. But to make it complete, really happy, I wanted eternal union with a man too: another kind of love.

Here Birkin is thinking unlike Tom Brangwen, but presumably rather like Lawrence himself. He is not necessarily implying that this would be a sexual relationship. However, he recognizes that 'it had been a necessity inside him all his life – to love a man purely and fully' in exactly the way he had loved Gerald Crich. Although the two of them enjoyed close physical contact in the episode in which they wrestled naked together, from Birkin's point of view, this relationship fell slightly short of the fully sworn and committed '**Blutbrüderschaft**' because Gerald 'kept his reserve. He held himself back.' Then with Gerald's death, even this less than completely satisfactory relationship has been taken from him.

KEYWORD

Blutbrüderschaft: means 'blood-brotherhood'. Two men who were actually unrelated would swear to act as brothers towards each other. This does not imply any sexual relationship.

Although Ursula and Birkin feel irritated with each other from time to time and experience conflict, they are able to get beyond this. At one point Ursula feels 'strictly hostile' to Birkin but like her grandfather she realizes that 'she was held to him by some bond, some deep principle' and it is this which 'saved her.' They are also very good for each other, Ursula rescuing Birkin from his occasional tendency to humourless stridency in perhaps the way Freida did for Lawrence himself.

THE HEALING POWER OF SEX

This is exemplified most clearly in the novels in the Ursula /Birkin and Connie/Mellors relationships; the latter appear to do better than the former. Connie and Mellors achieve simultaneous orgasm which is described in terms of a re-birth for Connie, she is a 'new-born thing.' Ursula and Birkin don't manage this, 'they were never *quite* together' – although there is a sense of optimism that this may come in the future. Both Ursula and Connie come with mixed feelings to anal intercourse, they appear passive acceptors rather than keen initiators. It says of Ursula that 'she gave way'; and of Connie that 'though a little frightened, she let him have his way.' Ursula, although uneasy about the fact that it might be regarded as 'bestial' or 'degraded', feels in the end that 'she was free, when she knew everything, and no dark shameful things were denied her.' For Connie the experience is 'burning out the shames, the deepest, oldest shames, in the most secret places.'

Both the Ursula/Birkin and Connie/Mellors relationships present matters principally from the woman's viewpoint. You could contrast this with a poem like 'Manifesto' where it is a man who is longing for the liberating touch of the woman's 'hand on my secret, darkest sources, the darkest outgoings.'

CONFLICT AND ANNIHILATION: DESTRUCTIVE RELATIONSHIPS

Lawrence sees relationships as failing either when one person, usually the woman, has a stronger personality than the other and cannot resist dominating and/or when one of the two is inadequate or overly needy in some way. A good example of the former is the **Oedipal** theme dealt with most famously in *Sons and Lovers*. In other novels there are examples of dominant woman playing a destructive role in heterosexual relationships.

The smothering mother

After her elder son's death, Mrs Morel in *Sons and Lovers* transfers her intense emotional needs and aspirations to her younger son, Paul, and cannot let him go to another woman. She doesn't really understand the Oedipal root of her dislike for Paul's girlfriend, Miriam: 'I'm sure I've tried to like her. I've tried and tried, but I can't – I can't.' But the result is that Mrs Morel controls Paul, he rather feebly succumbs to this and eventually comes to feel that it will never be possible for him to have a successful relationship with a woman while his mother lives. Interestingly, he and his mother are able to enjoy the close, easy physical intimacy which is completely lacking between Paul and Miriam. While having a conversation about Miriam 'he stroked his mother's hair, and his mouth was on her throat.' When Paul confesses 'Well, I don't love her, Mother,' Mrs Morel rewards her son by kissing 'him a long, fervent kiss.'

> **KEYWORD**
>
> Oedipal: refers to what is known as an Oedipus complex. This important idea in Freudian psychology postulates that a small boy, around the age of four or five, goes through a stage of feeling possessive, incestuous love for his mother and consequent jealousy of his father. The term gets its name from a well-known play by Sophocles in which Oedipus, separated from his mother at birth, later unknowingly returns to his land of origin to kill his father and marry his mother. The Oedipal period of development should, under normal circumstances, merely be an important but passing stage. If, however, the child becomes fixated on his mother at this point in time, it may later lead to an inability to form healthy adult relationships.

In the poem 'Monologue of a Mother', the narrator is in much the same situation as Mrs Morel at the end of the novel. Her third and last son has left and she feels she has little to live for, merely 'dead days fusing together in dross.' The son, although now freed, is emotionally crippled by their relationship:

> Like a bird from the far north blown with a broken wing
> Into our sooty garden, he drags and beats
> Along the fence perpetually, seeking release
> From me, from the hand of my love …

The well-known rhyming poem 'Piano', tells, with its initial lulling waltz rhythms and soft 's' sounds, of the dangerous way a grown man can be betrayed by sentimental longings for a return to the security of mother-love. The adult remembers crouching as a small child in a foetal position between his mother's feet as she played the piano: it was there he felt safe and loved.

The strong woman

Anna and Will's relationship in *The Rainbow*, in a chapter tellingly entitled 'Anna Vitrix' is a good example of a strong woman disabling her husband in a relationship. Anna's mother Lydia gives her daughter sound advice when Anna first encounters problems with Will:

> Between two people the love itself is the important thing, and that is neither you nor him. It is a third thing you must create. You mustn't expect it to be just in your way.

However, despite their brief initial blissful happiness, the pair seem unable to do this. Anna cannot resist manipulating Will and trying to dominate him; she actively enjoys the challenge, 'she was the enemy, very good,' and resists compromise. When he is annoyed that 'she had carelessly pushed away his tools so that they got rusty,' her response is the defiant, 'I shall leave them where I like.' She then deliberately chooses to use her sewing machine in the evening when she knows he cannot bear the sound. Having made her point she follows this up by sewing all day, ensuring that 'the whole house was covered with clipped calico' and making no effort to have his meal ready for him when he returns from work. Because she envies the pleasure he gets from illuminations in old missals and religious paintings, she ridicules them in order to destroy his enjoyment and satisfaction quite purposefully.

Eventually, Anna learns to get her satisfaction from 'her violent trance of motherhood'. Will gives up and gets on with the task of supporting a rapidly increasing family. He recognizes that 'she had conquered' – they will never succeed in reaching the ideal balance of two separate equals. He is sadly aware that he has 'failed to find expression ... in spirit he was uncreated.' Just as Alfred Brangwen before him, he diverts his feelings of frustration into flirting with another woman. Anna intuitively understands what he is up to and offers him an alternative: herself. The two find some sort of satisfaction in an arid passion of lust.

INADEQUACY

Other relationships fail because of some kind inadequacy in at least one of the partners. The Hermione/Birkin relationship in *Women in Love* is not dissimilar in some ways to that between Miriam and Paul in *Sons and Lovers*. Hermione lacks spontaneity. Birkin accuses her of wanting to have everything 'in your consciousness, make it all mental.' Miriam not only tends to do this, she also cannot find a balance in her relationship with Paul: 'She did not want to meet him so that there were two of them, man and woman together. She wanted to draw all of him into her.' Skrebensky in *The Rainbow* is both needy and unable to 'really want a woman, not with the whole of him: never love, never worship, only just physically want her?' Gerald Crich is also incapable of committing himself to the kind of relationship which Lawrence presents as the more ideal; like Skrebensky he acknowledges this: 'he would not make any pure relationship with any other soul. He could not.'

VIOLENCE

Violence between couples can reach savage proportions in Lawrence's fiction. This aggression is often described in sexual terms.

Both the Hermione/Birkin and Gerald/Gudrun relationships end with one of the pair feeling impelled to use a hideously murderous level of violence on the other. Both Hermione and Gerald feel simply that they must kill their partner in order to survive themselves, moreover they revel in the thought of violence which is described in terms of a sexual

satisfaction. Hermione waits until Birkin is sitting with his back to her engrossed in a book. She feels 'it must be done, or she must perish most horribly.' With 'a terrible voluptuous thrill' she takes up a heavy ball of lapis-lazuli and smashes it down on the back of Birkin's head. This gives her a feeling of 'unutterable satisfaction.' Similarly, in *Women in Love*, Gerald thinks 'what a perfect voluptuous consummation it would be to strangle her [Gudrun], to strangle every spark of life out of her, till she lay completely inert, soft, relaxed for ever, a soft heap lying dead between his hands, utterly dead.' When he actually attempts to put this plan into action 'a pure zest of satisfaction filled his soul.' Both Gerald and Gudrun are depicted as colluding in violence in such scenes as that with the pet rabbit and the one with the mare at the crossing gates discussed on page 26–7.

This theme occurs repeatedly in Lawrence's fiction. The story 'The Prussian Officer' is another good example of a relationship, this time between the captain and his orderly, which is based on an element of sado-masochism. When the captain hits the orderly in the face and sees 'the pain-tears in his eyes and the blood on his mouth' he feels 'a thrill of pleasure and of shame.' The poem 'Eloi, Eloi, Lama Sabachthani' is about a soldier who compares the man he is about to kill to a bride who 'took the blade of my bayonet, wanting it.' This makes the aggressor feel like the lover who has 'sown him with the seed / And planted and fertilised him.' However, in 'Love on the Farm', imagery from swordplay is used in the context of a sexual approach. Here the woman sits at home imagining her lover's masterful throttling of a rabbit before his return to her. She thrills to his arrival:

> ah! the uplifted sword
> Of his hand against my bosom! and oh, the broad
> Blade of his glance ...

She is conscious of 'his fingers that still smell grim / Of the rabbit's fur' as he strokes her face and there is a sense of excitement, not revulsion, as she appreciates this.

FULFILMENT THROUGH WORK

In order to be fully 'completed', Lawrence sees a person needing not only a fine relationship but also creative fulfilment through work and/or other aspects of their lives. In Lawrence's novels, characters tend to find satisfaction in working close to nature (for instance, Tom Brangwen, farming in *The Rainbow*, or Mellors, working as a gamekeeper in *Lady Chattterley's Lover*). Other careers, particularly those associated with industry, are something of a disaster. However, it is all a question of attitude. In the poem 'The Best of School', teaching is a rewarding experience; however, in 'Last Lesson of the Afternoon' it is something simply to be endured and survived – like Ursula's experiences at St Philip's.

In the poem 'We Are Transmitters', Lawrence writes of his ideal where the worker is creatively employed and so brings joy into the work:

> And if, as we work, we can transmit life into our work,
> life, still more life, rushes into us to compensate, to be ready
> and we ripple with life through the days.

'Things Men Have Made' is another poem in which Lawrence deals with satisfying employment. He describes craftsmen who have 'wakened hands' putting 'soft life' into their artefacts. The use of the tactile word 'soft' is echoed in Lawrence's admiration of the fact that these beautiful crafted objects are 'warm still' and 'glowing' with the 'transferred touch' of those who so lovingly made them. On the other hand, Lawrence expresses his dislike of mindless, mechanical, stultifying work as opposed to a more natural existence in such poems as 'Let Us Be Men' and 'City Life' as he does in several of his novels. The latter poem presents a particularly memorable image of the workers like 'hooked fishes' being pulled 'back and forth to work.'

It is clear Lawrence believes that forcing one's talent into an inappropriate direction has a truly corrosive effect on a person's ability to reach their full potential in every arena of life. In *The Rainbow*, Alfred, Tom Brangwen's older brother, has a real talent for drawing. He becomes a draughtsman in a lace factory, work which cramps his natural talent:

> … at drawing, his hand swung naturally in big, bold lines, rather lax, so that it was cruel for him to pedgill away at the lace-designing, working from the tiny squares of paper, counting and plotting and niggling.

He sticks 'to his chosen lot, whatever it should cost.' As a consequence 'he came back into life set and rigid, a rare-spoken, almost surly man.' His son, Will, who shows some creative talent at wood-carving when he first meets his future wife, Anna, has this destroyed in him. This is partly because he follows his father's profession, finding it just as soul-destroying as his father had, and partly because of the unsatisfactory nature of his relationship with Anna.

Gerald Crich, in *Women in Love*, is a mine-owner. His father before him had run the enterprise on humanitarian lines but when Gerald takes over he has 'no emotional qualms'. He sees himself as being the 'controlling, central part' of a 'great social productive machine.' With brutal efficiency he re-organizes the business without regard to what he sees as 'sentimental humanitarianism.' Indeed the whole business is rendered so frighteningly efficient that Gerald himself is almost superfluous to the whole operation and he starts to feel empty and afraid. When his father is sick and dying, he seeks relief from these feelings in a relationship with Gudrun – but he has become the sort of person who cannot really give himself in a relationship. His spiritual growth has been atrophied – like Sir Clifford in *Lady Chatterley's Lover*.

NATURAL GROWTH V. INDUSTRIALIZATION

This moves us naturally onto the next theme. It is clear that when Lawrence was a child growing up in a miner's family, he regarded colliers as being quite a part of the natural world still, even though their work took them underground. This view is evident in the early novel, *Sons and Lovers* where the mine workings make 'queer mounds and little black places among the corn-fields and the meadows.' They are there, but they are not intrusive, they blend fairly happily into the countryside. Similarly 'the cottages of these coalminers, in blocks and pairs here and there' fit in seamlessly with 'odd farms and homes of the stockingers, straying over the parish'.

After a short absence abroad with Freida, Lawrence returned to England and was repelled by the sort of efficient advances in industry characterized by Gerald Crich. His disgust at the repellent nature of a modern colliery town where the natural world has more or less been edged out altogether is evident in his description of Wiggiston in *The Rainbow*:

> The streets were like visions of pure ugliness; a grey-black macadamized road, asphalt causeways, held in between a flat succession of wall, window, and door, a new-brick channel that began nowhere, and ended nowhere. Everything was amorphous, yet everything repeated itself endlessly. Only now and then, in one of the house-windows vegetables or small groceries were displayed for sale.

This appalling environment affects the people living there who seem 'not like living people but like spectres.'

The same horror at modern industrialization and its effects on both the people and the landscape are evident in the strongly worded poem

'The North Country'. This poem builds a relentlessly powerful picture, emphasized by solid rhythm and rhyme. The people of the north are sunk into a hypnotic stupor by the works which rule their lives:

> Out of the sleep, from the gloom of motion, soundlessly somnambulent
> Moans and booms the soul of a people imprisoned, asleep in the rule
> Of the strong machine that runs mesmeric, booming the spell of its word
> Upon them and moving them helpless, mechanic, their will to its will deferred.

On the other hand, growing up at one with the natural world clearly has an enriching and soothing effect on the human spirit. One of the best examples of this is the oft-quoted, beautifully written passage in *The Rainbow* where Tom, on the night of his son's birth, takes his step-daughter Anna into the barns for a nightly check on the livestock. The little girl is hysterical and beside herself with grief: she does not understand why her mother cannot put her to bed as usual. He carries the child into 'the high, dry barn, that smelled warm even if it were not warm … They were in another world now.' The comforting atmosphere, the rhythmic movements and sounds of 'the snuffing and breathing of cows', 'the soft, steady light' all serve to quieten the child. It is evident from the sheer beauty of so many of Lawrence's natural descriptions, whether in prose or verse, that he himself was an acute observer of the natural world who took great joy from it.

❋ ❋ ❋ SUMMARY ❋ ❋ ❋

● Lawrence's writing centres around the idea of polarity. His themes include:

● Finding a balanced relationship. Although couples will need to work through conflict in order to achieve this, a fulfilling, balanced, mutually respectful sexual relationship is one of the few healing balms for the human spirit.

● Conflict – the destructive potential of relationships, whether mother/son or straightforwardly heterosexual. When a relationship goes badly wrong it can be an annihilating force for an individual.

● Fulfilment through work.

● The natural as opposed to the industrial world.

7 Contemporary critical approaches

The late Edwardian society of which Lawrence was part, was both deeply traditional and highly conventional. There was a strong feeling amongst many educated men that they had a duty, in their superior learned wisdom, to ensure that the reading matter available to women, servants and the lower and middle-class working masses was of an appropriate kind. In 1909, representatives of Boots the Chemists, who had a huge lending library system within their stores, and W. H. Smith, whose news stalls appeared on most railway stations, joined with *The Times* Book Club and others to form a Circulating Libraries' Association. They agreed it was their clear moral duty not to make available any material which might offend their readership by what they judged to be 'scandalous, libellous, immoral or otherwise disagreeable' contents. They expected publishers to submit any dubious material to them for vetting prior to its publication. Despite objections from some publishers, this was generally agreed to be a thoroughly good move.

We must remember that literary criticism operated in an entirely different way in Lawrence's day. University academics were not, on the whole, engaged in serious, considered studies of authors. There was no range of specialist academic journals available. To be reviewed was to have a commentary printed in a newspaper or perhaps in the *Athenaeum,* an arts magazine for the intelligentsia with a relatively limited circulation.

Contemporary criticism of Lawrence fell broadly into three sequential bands. The first, a response to his first three novels and early poetry, largely saw him as showing great promise. The second, following and during the publication of his other work, tended to lack comprehension of it and express dismay at the appalling waste of talent employed in such a thoroughly tasteless way. In August 1921, John Middleton Murry, a close friend of Lawrence's in his life-time, actually accused him of having 'murdered his gifts' in an article in *Nation and Athenaeum*. The third involved a largely disapproving analysis of the psychology of the author.

INITIAL CRITICAL REACTION: EARLY POETRY, *THE WHITE PEACOCK, THE TRESPASSER*

Key critical attitudes were apparent immediately on first publication. Early reviewers recognized the genius of the writer (genius became the favourite label to apply to Lawrence) and admired his descriptive powers, particularly of the natural world. But there was also a persistent puzzlement, a sense of uncertainty and unease, both about his written style and about the author himself.

As early as December 1909, Henry Yoxall, writing in the *Schoolmaster*, hailed Lawrence delightedly as a 'true-born poet' and compared him favourably with Walt Whitman. Other reviewers of his poetry remarked appreciatively on the power and fresh intensity of his poetry. However, the unsigned contributor to the *Nation* of November 1914, did include, in an otherwise enthusiastic review, a comment on the 'strangeness' of the verse.

This tone was taken up and echoed by the reviewers of the first two novels. The author of the unsigned review in the *Morning Post* of February 1911 admired the lyricism of the writing but wondered what social class the writer of *The White Peacock* could have emerged from. He questioned the authenticity of cottagers earnestly engaged in conversation about Ibsen and Aubrey Beardsley and, interestingly, pondered the sex of the author. Allan Monkhouse, writing in the *Manchester Guardian* of February 1911, also used the word 'lyrical' to describe Lawrence's prose and felt that he showed enormous promise – 'but promise of what we are not quite able to define.' He, too, questioned the intellectual interests of the characters and wondered whether the hero's experience of having French and Latin talked at him by Letty, together with discussing Strauss and Debussy whilst trying to run a pub, might quite understandably have driven him to drink. The anonymous contributor to a February 1911 edition of the *Daily News* admired the eloquent flow of the novel and conceded that it certainly cast a kind of 'spell' on the reader – although he had reservations about the inclusion of such frank, unpleasant and graphic detail as those given on a cat caught in a trap and that on the killing of rabbits and mice.

Reviews of *The Trespasser* continued in the same vein. Basil de Selincourt, writing in the *Manchester Guardian* of June 1912, admired both the poetic quality of the descriptions and the psychological accuracy with which the two main characters were drawn. The unsigned contributor to the *Morning Post,* writing in the same month, felt that the novel was 'remarkable.' He did, however, add the caveat that this novel, like the last, dealt with 'abnormal persons'.

REACTION TO *SONS AND LOVERS*

Reaction to *Sons and Lovers*, although largely very appreciative, developed along similar lines. Critics admired the delicacy with which Lawrence treated some characters and incidents in the novel. Although the contributor to the June 1913 *Saturday Review* felt that there was something 'strange' about Lawrence's writing, he particularly selected for favourable comment both the portrait of Morel and the episode in which Paul and Miriam climb the ruined tower. He felt that the natural delicacy with which Paul thinks to hold down Miriam's skirts for her as they ascend is tenderly and vividly portrayed. However, we can see in a copy of *The Westminster Gazette* a foreshadowing of things to come. This anonymous contributor, writing in 1913, although recognizing the haunting quality of the fiction, saying that it is 'a book to waylay the mind', points out that this novel does not have a 'hero', at least in the old-fashioned sense. The central character is not one whom we might necessarily wish to emulate, he is a sensitive being whose thoughts and feelings are expected to interest the reader.

The Oedipal aspect of Paul and Mrs Morel's relationship was understood, although the English translation of Freud's *Interpretation of Dreams* was published after the novel. Harold Massingham, writing in a June 1913 edition of the *Daily Chronicle* felt that the character of Paul suffered because he was too much a projection of Lawrence's own personality. He recommended the novel though, feeling it was by far the best of Lawrence's three to date. A contributor to the *Athanaeum* of June 1913 also felt that the author was over-involved in the character of Paul and therefore biased in his presentation of Miriam whom he had dealt with unfairly. John Middleton Murry developed the same idea a little later, just after Lawrence's death. In *Son of Woman*, published in 1931, Murry, a friend of Lawrence's, pursued the idea of how far Lawrence was telling the 'truth' in his writing. He felt that Lawrence had been unjust to the girl on whom Miriam was based. Of course it is perfectly true that Jessie Chambers had felt very hurt and wronged by her portrayal in this novel, but this complete identification of the real with the fictional was not necessarily entirely helpful in judging the quality of the fiction.

Wyndham-Lewis, in his *Paleface*, published in 1929, expressed disgust at how near to incest the theme of *Sons and Lovers* was. However, Alfred Booth Kuttner, writing in the *Psychoanalytic Review* of July, 1916, was fascinated by how closely *Sons and Lovers* echoed Freud's ideas. He approached the novel with real enthusiasm, feeling it offered a much more satisfactory opportunity to analyse feelings and motives than if they had been presented in the form of a real person. The printed page remained fixed and presented plenty of material for study, whereas a living subject could be evasive or irritatingly inarticulate about their emotions. Kuttner then engaged in an interesting and detailed analysis of Paul's Oedipal feelings and an explanation of why Paul, in his particular circumstances, was more paralysed by them than most. He pointed out that the universal existence of these feelings, although they would be felt and recognized more by some individuals than others, accounted both for the strong appeal and what he saw as the usefully

cathartic effect of this novel. Kuttner guessed that Lawrence may have written so well and with such involvement on this subject because he had experienced the feelings of the main character, but approached this in a most gentlemanly way, pointing out that no positive assumptions could safely be made without the author's willing co-operation. This refreshingly decent approach stands in stark contrast to many more modern critics who seem to have felt they could make the most preposterous assumptions about the alliance of Lawrence's life with his art with total impunity.

KEYWORD

Catharsis: is a term used by Aristotle in his *Poetics*. This Greek word literally means 'purgation'. Aristotle developed the idea that great tragic drama had certain characteristics, one of which was that it would arouse tremendously strong emotions of pity and fear in the spectator. Watching the play would have a therapeutic effect on the audience, who would leave the theatre at the end of the performance purged of these emotions.

RESPONSE TO *THE RAINBOW* AND *WOMEN IN LOVE*

Critical disillusion with Lawrence is painfully evident in the response to these two novels. Attack came on four main fronts: those who objected to the explicit descriptions of sex; those who found the anti-war sentiments in *The Rainbow* unpalatable; those who, without the benefit of Lawrence's explanation of what he was trying to achieve in Garnett, found the characters, particularly those in *Women in Love*, unsatisfactory and those who made personal attacks on Lawrence the man. In addition, there was some carping at Lawrence's style. Even Catherine Carswell, a friend of Lawrence's, who wrote one of the very few largely favourable reviews of *The Rainbow* which appeared in *The Glasgow Herald* in November 1915, mentioned her discomfort at the author's 'distressing tendency to the repetition of certain words and a curiously vicious rhythm into which he constantly falls in the more emotional passages.'

DISGUST AT SEXUAL DETAIL

The Rainbow was published in England by Methuen in September 1915 and banned on the grounds of obscenity only two months later. Even before the trial there was a note of hysteria in reviews. There was a feeling that the sexual detail was entirely gratuitous and that the desire to include it cast the author in an unfavourable light. Robert Lynd, writing in an October 1915 edition of the *Daily News* advised the 'ordinary' reader – by which he plainly meant 'one of normal, civilized tastes' – to leave the book well alone as it would be bound to offend any sense of decency, being as it was 'a monotonous wilderness of phallicism.' Clement Shorter, contributing to an edition of the *Sphere* in the same month, was also unsettled by the explicit nature of the sexual descriptions, particularly in the lesbian episode. He summarized the whole book as 'an orgie [sic] of sexiness'. James Douglas, writing at the same time in the *Star*, vented his disgust in no uncertain terms and had a good deal to say on the subject of the sacred 'responsibility of the artist', which he felt Lawrence had utterly failed to shoulder.

One of the chapters held up for particular criticism at the trial as likely to deprave and corrupt was that in which Ursula has 'the few months of intimacy' with her teacher, Winifred Inger. The other was that in which Ursula and Skrebensky make love for the last time on the dunes. Mr Muskett, prosecuting counsel at the trial, referred to the novel as 'this bawdy volume', whilst the magistrate, Sir John Dickinson, described it as 'utter filth'. Although Lawrence completed an early version of *Women in Love* in 1916, he failed to find a publisher in the wake of the controversy over *The Rainbow*. *Women in Love* had to wait until 1920 for publication, and then came out only in America; it appeared in England a year later.

Critics continued to be appalled by the sexual frankness of *Women in Love*. The anonymous contributor to the July 1921 *Saturday Westminster Gazette* pointed out wittily, but disapprovingly, that Lawrence's characters in *Women in Love* were prone to divest themselves quite gratuitously of their clothing at every available opportunity:

> Not only do all the heroes and heroines of this crowded tale cast off clothing whenever there is an excuse ... but they do it unexpectedly – at garden parties (Gudrun and Ursula) – after dinner, over their cigarettes (Birkin and Crich), while talking round the fire on a winter morning (ever so many people), for no revealed purpose so far as their consequent actions are recorded.

This critic also objected to what he felt was the coarse language chosen to describe the naked human body: 'he chooses the vocabulary of the butcher's shop in preference to that of the anatomy class.' John Middleton Murry, writing in the *Athenaeum* of August 1921, described the novel as 'deliberately, incessantly, and passionately obscene.' Although he criticizes Lawrence for his 'passionate vehemence' in this novel, it is exactly that strident quality in the review which strikes a reader most forcibly. It is thought that Lawrence had suggested that he and Murry indulge in exactly the sort of loving but not actively homosexual relationship which Birkin wants to achieve with Gerald in *Women in Love.* Murry rejected the idea. Some of his distaste and unease emerges in his writing.

DISLIKE OF UNPATRIOTIC SENTIMENTS

It was perhaps characteristic of Lawrence's sometimes wilful intransigence that he expected a novel so explicitly anti-war as *The Rainbow* to be accepted so readily on publication at that particular point in British history: a year after the beginning of the First World War. Lawrence was known not to support the Allied cause in the war. He had a German wife and had even dedicated the novel to his sister-in-law, Else, in German. Reviewers distrusted the appearance of these sentiments at such a sensitive moment. James Douglas, writing in *The Star* in the review mentioned above, said quite frankly that such a book had 'no right to exist in the wind of war.' The magistrate presiding over the case at Bow Street Court in 1915 had lost his son in action only weeks before hearing the case.

By the time *Women in Love* appeared, Lawrence had apparently repudiated his native land in favour of a life abroad. This, together with the apparent relish with which he depicts the collapse of English society in that novel, combined to make him appear particularly suspect. John Middleton Murry, who had been a War Office censor, claimed to have the public interest at heart when taking up particular, disapproving attitudes to these novels and referring to Lawrence as an 'outlaw' of English literature. Murry felt that every author had certain understood responsibilities and duties to his readers and that Lawrence had abandoned these. Both he and Wyndham-Lewis felt that Lawrence's writings demonstrated unhealthy and sinister Bolshevist tendencies. He was patently trying to undermine wholesome British culture. Wyndham-Lewis felt that Lawrence should be regarded with fear and suspicion as the most dangerous anti-Western propagandist in existence.

UNSATISFACTORY CHARACTERIZATION

Critics found many of the characters in the two novels unappealing, unconvincing or both. The author of an unattributed review in the *Athenaeum* of November 1915 thought that the minor characters in *The Rainbow* were reasonably convincing but that Lawrence had failed to deal adequately with the principals. He argued that Lawrence had decided, against any consideration of probability, to introduce a Polish aristocrat into the Cossethay locality to meet and marry a representative of English yeoman stock and had then failed to deal realistically with such a union. John Middleton Murry, in *Son of Woman* (1931) asserted quite categorically that Ursula was, in *The Rainbow,* 'an unconvincing character.'

However, it was *Women in Love* which came in for the most thorough-going criticism on the character front. The unnamed critic, writing in the *Saturday Westminster Gazette* of July 1921, felt that Lawrence's main male characters, Birkin and Gerald, were indistinguishable in terms of their personality; by the end of the novel they 'lose their identities and become one and the same young man.' He felt that the same applied to Ursula and Gudrun – although they could at least be identified by the different coloured stockings which they chose to wear. John Middleton Murry, writing in the *Athanaeum* of August 1921, made a similar point even more strongly. He argued that the male characters were completely indistinguishable from the female in this novel – apart from the tediously and unnecessarily detailed items of clothing with which they were adorned at least some of the time. He also could find no difference whatever in the love experiences of the two pairs of lovers, Gerald/Gudrun and Birkin/Ursula and was, therefore, at a loss to understand why the first couple ended up so disastrously whilst the second enjoyed rapturous bliss.

LADY CHATTERLEY'S LOVER

Since this novel was banned in England for 32 years after its first publication in Italy, there was not a plethora of English reviewers of it in Lawrence's life-time. A notable exception is the well-known unsigned contribution to an October 1928 edition of *John Bull*. This writer was objecting in the strongest possible terms to the fact that this novel could in fact be obtained, at a price and under the counter, from certain booksellers. The tone is highly emotive and vituperative; it accuses Lawrence of having a 'diseased mind' and, using a high-minded and patriotic tone, refers to the novel both as 'the most evil outpouring that has ever besmirched the literature of our country' and 'the fetid masterpiece of this sex-sodden genius.' Note, however, the familiar reference to genius. The reviewer does put Lawrence, as an analyst of human psychology, in 'the front rank of living writers.' And there was an occasional lone voice raised in support of this novel. W. B. Yeats, at least, appreciated Lawrence's intentions. In a letter to Olivia Shakespear written in May 1933, Yeats observed that 'the coarse language' of Mellors 'becomes a forlorn poetry uniting their [his and Connie's] solitudes, something ancient, humble and terrible.'

OBITUARIES

Obituaries tended to take the now familiar line that Lawrence, the man of genius, had not lived up to his early promise. There were the usual tributes to his powers and the oft-reiterated criticisms of what were perceived as weaknesses and preoccupations. Two, however, stand out, partly because the writers were eminent in their own right and partly because they did pay largely unqualified tribute to Lawrence. Arnold Bennett, writing in the *Evening Standard* of 10 April 1930, declared staunchly that in his view, Lawrence was 'no more obsessed by sex than any normal human being.' He admired the range and honesty of Lawrence's work. However, he did cavil, as others had, with Lawrence's tendency to repeat himself, feeling it was 'extravagant and indisciplined.' E. M. Forster, contributing to *The Listener* of 30 April 1930, paid tribute to the 'tenderness' of Lawrence's writing and expressed regret that he was 'not being read enough or in the right way.'

LAWRENCE – A DEPLORABLE PERSONALITY

Contemporary criticism of Lawrence often served to imply that Lawrence the man was sadly deficient in order to write in the way that he had in these novels. However, immediately after his death this kind of approach reached new heights. The two critics most responsible, John Middleton Murry and T. S. Eliot, were eminent literary figures: their words carried weight. In the case of Murry, there was in addition the fact that he had (sadly, in view of the tenor of his writing) been Lawrence's friend.

Murry's study of Lawrence's novels, *Son of Woman* (1931) was both completely damning and very influential. Murry took the same strident line as he had in his earlier reviews of Lawrence's work. He pursued the not unusual approach at the time of examining the psychology of the author in order to account for his writing. He saw Lawrence as dominated by his mother who made him feel deeply ashamed of his sexual feelings and made him repress them. Lawrence therefore had to resort to fantasy in order to see himself as the kind of wild, dominant, virile figure which he could never be in real life. Murray saw *Sons and Lovers* as a part of this fantasy life: Lawrence vicariously reaching independence through his fictional character.

However, in *The Rainbow*, Murry saw Lawrence re-creating his own sexual failure with Freida and his fear of a powerfully dominant woman in the relationships of Anna/Will and Skrebensky/Ursula. Thereafter, Murry thought Lawrence's aggressive wish to be revenged on dominant females even more pronounced. In *Women in Love*, he has Birkin (who is really Lawrence himself) annihilate the overly demanding Ursula whom he cannot satisfy. Once this is done, Birkin can complete her humiliation by forming an alliance with another man.

T. S. Eliot, writing in *After Strange Gods* (1934), took up the most lamentably superior intellectual stance. He felt that Lawrence, having been deprived of the intellectual rigours of a reasonable education, but subject to the influence of Protestant pieties, had not been given any decent guiding principles or developed critical faculties. Nevertheless, Eliot recognized the power of Lawrence's message and, like Murry and Wyndham Lewis, feared its likely debilitating effect on young, impressionable minds.

Thanks to these critics, it became fashionable to deride Lawrence, whose literary reputation was to remain in the doldrums for years, until rescued by F. R. Leavis. Still, had Lawrence been observing from beyond the grave, he might have taken comfort from this remark attributed to Jonathan Swift: 'When a true genius appears in the world, you may know him by this sign, that all the dunces are all in confederacy against him.'

❋ ❋ ❋ SUMMARY ❋ ❋ ❋

- Early reaction to Lawrence saw him as a writer of great genius and promise, albeit rather strange.

- Lawrence irrevocably offended with *The Rainbow, Women in Love* and *Lady Chatterley's Lover*.

- By the time of his death, fear and dislike characterized the often vitriolic views of eminent critics.

8 Modern critical approaches

For two decades after his death in 1930, Lawrence was unfashionable, regarded as unworthy of serious attention. The few publications on him remained steadfastly concerned with the author's own history and psychology.

THE 1950s

In 1955 F. R. Leavis published *D. H. Lawrence: Novelist*, and for the first time Lawrence was presented as a thoroughly worthy, moral writer. Leavis argued that there was a definable canon of great English literature in which Lawrence had a place. In order to establish Lawrence's genius as an undoubted part of the literary good and great, Leavis spent much time comparing him favourably with George Eliot.

However, Leavis saw Lawrence as writing at a much higher level of poetic intensity than that of which Eliot was capable. He cited, amongst other examples, the description in *The Rainbow* of Lydia seen by Tom through a window nursing her child as he arrives to court her at the vicarage. Leavis pointed out that this is a completely unsentimental picture of a mother and child, devoid of any clichés. Lydia is described tenderly, reverently and with a sense of wonder which makes the picture live in the mind of the reader. Leavis disagreed with Murry that Lawrence was unable to present credible characters, arguing that he was in fact a master of convincing characterization.

Leavis's perceptions clearly owed a debt to the 'Lawrence the man' school of thought but served to realign attention away from the author to the text. His work created a burgeoning of academic and critical interest in Lawrence, who was seen at last as a novelist of stature. Infinitely more was written on Lawrence in the second half of the 50s than had been produced in the whole 20 years immediately after his death.

THE 1960s

The prosecution of *Lady Chatterley's Lover* in 1960 helped to focus the attention of people generally on Lawrence; it gave a massive boost to sales of all his novels in England and abroad. Public opinion had finally caught up with Lawrence: he seemed the prophet of the 60s, the writer who spoke for an age which had come to value sexual and personal freedoms. In his poem 'Annus Mirabilis', printed in *High Windows*, Philip Larkin summed up Lawrence's place in the mood of the time:

> Sexual intercourse began
> In nineteen sixty-three
> (Which was rather late for me) –
> Between the end of the Chatterley ban
> And the Beatles' first LP.

Lawrence was deemed sufficiently establishment to appear on the A-Level syllabus for the first time. He has since become a regular feature of public and undergraduate examinations.

LAWRENCE THE ESTABLISHMENT FIGURE

The massive revival of interest in Lawrence came only a little before something of a revolution in literary criticism. It was no longer sufficient to concentrate on textual analysis as Leavis had done. The text was now viewed through a range of different approaches which have come to be known under the heading of 'Theory'. These different approaches include **post-structuralism**, **Marxism**, **feminism** and **psychoanalytical criticism**.

KEYWORDS

Feminism: in literature focuses on the experience of women, particularly in the novel. A feminist approach to *Sons and Lovers* finds gender and sexuality to be the guiding principles in the novel.

Marxism: in literature indicates that the writer is writing from the standpoint of Marx's philosophical ideas which take the class struggle to be fundamental to history. Thus a Marxist interpretation of *Sons and Lovers* will focus on the difference of social class between Paul's parents as an explanation for his difficulties and attitudes.

Post-structuralism: tends to reveal that the meaning of any text is inherently unstable. It is a rather loose term which refers to the process of deconstructing the text.

Psychoanalytical criticism: stems from Freud's study of personality. The psychoanalytical approach to *Sons and Lovers* will see Paul's Oedipal relationship with his mother as central to the novel.

POST-STRUCTURALISM

Roland Barthes was a particularly important influence in post-structuralism. The author was never again going to be seen as the 'explanation' of the work after the publication of Barthes's essay 'Death of the Author' in 1968. This postulated two very interesting and influential ideas. One was that since the reader could never be relied upon to have the same mental concept of any given word as the author, all meaning in a text was inherently unreliable and unstable. A second was that the authority of authors must be questioned because they often do not fully understand what they are doing; there is often a considerable discrepancy between an author's intentions and the results. This idea is interestingly close to what Lawrence himself said, 45 years earlier, quoted in *Studies in Classic American Literature*, (Penguin, 1977):

> The artist usually sets out – or used to – to point a moral and adorn a tale. The tale, however, points the other way, as a rule ... Never trust the artist. Trust the tale. The proper function of a critic is to save the tale from the artist who created it.

THE FEMINIST APPROACH

Feminist critics have had a great deal to say about Lawrence in recent decades. Response has, however, been ambivalent. On the one hand Lawrence does express a good deal of anger at women in his writing: it appears he was fascinated by a particularly dominant, independent type of woman on whom he took a kind of literary revenge in his novels. On the other hand, Lawrence can be seen as a liberating force for women.

Hilary Simpson in *D. H. Lawrence and Feminism* (Northern Illinois University Press, 1982), points out that Lawrence's writing was very much influenced by the first explosion of the women's movement in his own time. She also argues that the first to put the feminist case against Lawrence was Murry in *Son of Woman* (1931). Murry presented a picture of Lawrence, who, because he was insecure and inadequate, needed to annihilate powerful, demanding women in his fiction and establish a 'sexual mystery beyond the phallic, wherein he is lord.' Simpson goes on to say that the two early classic statements of the feminist position, Simone de Beauvoir's *The Second Sex* (trans. H. M. Pashley, Jonathan Cape, 1953) and Kate Millett's *Sexual Politics* (Hart-Davis, 1977), were following in a line carved for them by Murry.

In fact it may be more likely that Millett was partly reacting against critics (largely male) who, in the late 60s and early 70s, had been copious in their praise of Lawrence as an author who thoroughly understood the female psyche. H. M. Daleski, in *The Forked Flame: A Study of D. H. Lawrence* (Faber and Faber, 1965), had stated that 'Lawrence was a woman in a man's skin' in order to describe Lawrence's ability to empathize with the female point of view. Norman Mailer, in *The Prisoner of Sex* (Sphere, 1972), said that 'Lawrence understood women as they had never been understood before.'

Kate Millett

Millett has very strongly held opinions which are immediately evident to the reader. She believes that Lawrence writes from a relentlessly autobiographical point of view and presents this in rather unquestioning black and white terms: for example, she thinks that the portrait of Connie Chatterley is one of Lawrence's mother as he would have liked her to be and that Lawrence is fulsomely describing his own intimate anatomy in the details he gives of Mellors's penis.

It is also immediately apparent which novels Millett likes and which she dislikes. One cannot escape feeling that she likes, on the whole, those novels which she feels promote an attitude towards women of which she can approve, and dislikes those which do not. For instance, the author clearly enjoys the first two-thirds of *The Rainbow* but finds the latter third, together with *Women in Love* and much of *Lady Chatterley's Lover* deeply irritating. She sees the first part of *The Rainbow* as satisfying, dominated by the matriarchal attitudes of Lydia and Anna; these two women, she thinks, conquer their men. She also enjoys the vibrant sense of first-hand experience in *Sons and Lovers* in passages such as those describing Mrs Morel's routine or William's funeral – although since Millett perceives Paul as an arrogant, selfish manipulator of women for his own ends, prone to discard them once they are no longer of service, she largely disapproves of this novel as well.

Nor does she think much of Ursula's promising to love, honour and obey Birkin and settle down as his little adjunct in *Women in Love*. She is even more outraged by *Lady Chatterley's Lover*, which she sees as being the story of the re-birth of Connie through her encounters with what Lawrence called 'the mystery of the phallus.' She objects to what she sees as the concentration on descriptions of male genitalia – she thinks this a tribute to the power of the penis – whilst there are relatively few details of female genitalia. Lawrence's inhibitions about women are behind this, she reasons, in addition to his innate feelings of attraction to other men. His interest in sodomy lies behind the details he gives of anal intercourse. She is critical of Mellors's disinclination to indulge Connie in foreplay and of Connie's lack of interest in a worthwhile independent career of her own.

Millett is well worth reading: she has a delightfully dry sense of humour and she gets you thinking and reacting, both to Lawrence and her opinions.

Feminist writing of the 1980s

Millett's very personal and angry interpretation was followed by more balanced, less vitriolic assessments in the 80s exemplified by both Hilary Simpson (see above), Carol Dix in *D. H. Lawrence and Women* (Macmillan, 1980) and Sheila MacLeod in her *Lawrence's Men and Women* (Heinemann, 1985). These are all well worth reading. The three authors mention Millett and their different degrees of discomfiture with her argument that Lawrence's writing degrades women. They challenge many of her assertions

Dix argues that Lawrence's presentation of Connie is actually liberating for women rather than degrading because it presents Connie joyously celebrating her own sexuality. The viewpoint of the novel is largely Connie's and she is 'allowed' to do the sorts of things which had previously been the bastions of male privilege in novels: she is free to adore and celebrate Mellors's naked body; when she feels like sex she can initiate it; she then thoroughly enjoys it. MacLeod points out that for Lawrence the phallus is not only a symbol of male potency but also his connection with a woman. Picking up on Millett's objection to the fact that Lawrence appears to use the word 'phallic' interchangeably with 'sexual' in *Lady Chatterley's Lover*, Simpson discusses Connie's identification with Mellors's penis as the instrument of her pleasure and her claim that she has a kind of ownership of it.

Of these three writers, it is perhaps Simpson's considered, scholarly approach, giving a historical context to the sexual politics, which most points the way forward to the 90s.

The 1990s and after

More recent feminist writing has tended to be less personal (we have moved a long way away from MacLeod's assertion that as the mother of two sons herself she simply cannot understand the pressure which Mrs Morel puts on Paul in *Sons and Lovers*). There is, however, still sometimes that familiar sense that female critics feel cheated by Lawrence. Elizabeth Fox, in a paper entitled 'Closure and Foreclosure in *The Rainbow*' published in *The D. H. Lawrence Review* (1997, v. 27, n. 2/3) discusses the ending of that novel. She comments on the symbolism in the final pages, using the evocative term 'cascade', taken from Lacan's *Ecrits: A Selection* (trans. Alan Sheridan, Norton, 1977), to convey the rich proliferation of images in the last two chapters. She considers the wealth of meanings surrounding the moon, the stampede of horses, the oak kernel and the rainbow in the light of ideas from psychoanalysis but concludes that the ending is something of a 'loss of quest': 'the text sacrifices Ursula's former pursuit of agency and substitutes for it a Handmaiden passively awaiting a Son of God.'

Other modern feminist writing has clearly also been enriched and informed by diverse academic interests. One example of this is Linda Ruth Williams, who brings an expertise in film studies to enhance her arguments in *Sex in the Head: Visions of Femininity and Film in D. H. Lawrence* (Wayne State University Press, 1993), and *D. H. Lawrence* (Northcote Publishers, 1997). Another is Barbara Ann Schapiro, who takes a psychoanalytic perspective in *D. H. Lawrence and the Paradoxes of Psychic Life* (State University of New York Press, 1999). Although approaching their study of Lawrence from rather different standpoints, both authors focus to an extent on the sado-masochistic elements in Lawrence. Try to read these authors in full yourself: there is no space to give justice to the complexity and depth of their arguments here.

Linda Ruth Williams

Williams refers to *Fantasia of the Unconscious/Psychoanalysis and the Unconscious* in which Lawrence develops his ideas about the development of the individual from infancy to maturity. She points out that several of Lawrence's more cerebral women are 'stuck' in an early voyeuristic stage of development; they cannot progress to a freeing, balanced relationship founded in a more instinctive response of 'letting go'. Individuals such as Gudrun and Hermione in *Women in Love* are prime examples of this 'female heterosexual sadism.' Their attitude to men is characterized by a voyeuristic attitude which is closely linked with aggression. She quotes many examples from the novel where one or other of these women are avid spectators of men, using the fact that Hermione 'loved to watch' and looked at Birkin with 'leering eyes.'

There are two fascinating concomitants here. One is that whereas feminism usually sees women as victims of the male gaze, Lawrence is reversing this and seeing certain women as empowered in this way. The second is that it is the very type of woman whom Lawrence seemed to distrust, his 'cocksure women' who are described in these terms. Williams points out that much as he dislikes them, Lawrence can't resist returning to them again and again – and destroying them.

Barbara Ann Schapiro and psychoanalysis

Barbara Schapiro's thought-provoking psychcoanalytic interpretation of Lawrence, *D. H. Lawrence and the Paradoxes of Psychic Life* (State University of New York Press, 1999), concentrates on the short stories together with three novels: *Sons and Lovers, The Rainbow* and *Women in Love.* The author points out that in some ways psychoanalytical theory has only just caught up with some of Lawrence's insights into human nature. She deals most interestingly with the way in which several of Lawrence's characters appear to practise what is termed 'mirroring' in modern jargon. In other words, the characteristic which a person objects to most violently in someone else is one which they themselves share and actually dislike in themselves. Thus, Paul in *Sons and Lovers* sees in Miriam his own (and his mother's) inhibitions and stunted emotional life; he hates and resents this in her. Both Clara and Paul accuse each other of being unable to recognize and cope with the real person that is them. They both fear that the other will be unable to deal with or love the vulnerable, damaged person that they each know themselves to be inside.

Schapiro develops the idea that individuals feel a need or as Lawrence often describes it, an 'emptiness' inside them which they try to assuage by a relationship or by some other method – Walter Morel eventually dulls his 'emptiness, almost like a vacuum in his soul' by drink. Mrs Morel is haunted by a neediness created by her unloving and harsh father. This was exacerbated first by the fact that she was rejected by the man she loved and then by her disappointments in the man she did marry. Let down by a series of men, she is embittered and depressive. Because Mrs Morel is not in touch with her own emotions and feelings, Paul, who idolizes her, follows the same pattern.

Another pattern picked up by this author is the way in which men come to hate women once they realize how vulnerable they are. As a child, Paul hates his sister's doll once he has broken it just as he hates Miriam as soon as he perceives he has hurt her. Morel hates his wife once he has thrown the drawer at her. In *The Rainbow* Will Brangwen evidences an intermittently sadistic attitude to his small daughter Ursula. Her sensitivity and vulnerability infuriate him because they remind him of his own.

Schapiro has a great deal of time for Lawrence's idea that individuals are best able to achieve a relationship when they can respect each other as individuals and achieve a good balance with each other. She deals both in the book mentioned above and in her paper 'Transitional States and Psychic Change' in *Contemporary Psychoanalysis* (January, 1999), with the scene in *The Rainbow* where Tom takes Anna into the barn on the night of her step-brother's birth. She points out that it is only when Tom stops fighting against Lydia's separateness, her withdrawal into labour, that he can relax and begin to move on and change. Once he allows Lydia her separate existence then he can recognize her nurturing role in himself and use this to soothe Anna. He can get in touch with his own feelings of anger whilst allowing the child to express hers freely. Schapiro sees the relationship between Ursula and Birkin working in *Women in Love* because although they can and do each assert themselves against the other, after the anger is over neither is destroyed and they still both need and want the other. They accept each other as they are without idealization. This is, of course, very unlike the relationship between Ursula and Skrebensky in *The Rainbow*.

OTHER READINGS OF LAWRENCE

The Marxist/materialist view

Graham Holderness, in his book *D. H. Lawrence: History, Ideology and Fiction* (Gill and Macmillan, 1982), uses as one of his starting points Terry Eagleton's short but inspiring treatment of Lawrence in *Ideology and Criticism* (NLB, 1976). Here Eagleton argues that in one way *The Rainbow* is 'ultra-realist.' Holderness challenges this idea of *The Rainbow* as social history; instead he sees the novel developed around a series of **myths**.

> **KEYWORD**
>
> **Myth:** is a fiction concerned with creation and explains how something came to exist. James Joyce relied on mythical material in *Ulysses*.

Holderness thinks it unhelpful to regard Wiggiston at the end of the novel as a real place. He points out that the descriptive details of the town are 'not at all realist in manner': they are meant to conjure up the intensity of a nightmare which is Ursula's state of mind at that point in time. He reads the fact that we are told there is 'a large, open, shapeless space' at the centre of the town as crucial. He suggests that we should read the novel 'backwards' and see Marsh Farm as a myth designed to 'fill that blank space in the centre of Wiggiston' because the farm represents the antithesis of Wiggiston in terms of values and attitudes. In order to support his contention that we should see Marsh Farm in terms of myth rather than reality, Holderness points out that we do not see the farm as part of a rural community. There appear to be no other workers on the farm; those who live there do not interact with local people; even at a social occasion like the wedding, the guests are shadowy, unrealized presences. In Chapter 3 when Tom does go out into the local community, the experience is described from the point of view of the young Anna who is an outsider, looking on with 'a radically alienated perspective.'

Holderness's conclusion is that Lawrence lost more than he gained by abandoning realism in favour of myth in *The Rainbow*. He appears to prefer a novel like *Sons and Lovers*, which is, in his view, a more realist novel that responds more fruitfully to historical analysis.

The sub-text

Modern criticism has interested itself as much in the gaps as the presences of a text. Terry Eagleton, in his informative text, *Literary Theory: An Introduction* (Oxford, 1983), pays attention to the form of *Sons and Lovers*, examining what he calls the 'sub-text'. He points out that all novels contain at least one sub-text, and these can be seen as the 'unconscious' of the work: 'what it does not say, and *how* it does not say it, may be as important as what it articulates.' In other words, in the case of this work, he argues that a novel featuring such a confused central character provides us with a degree of ambivalence which may be of central importance to a full understanding of it.

This point in relation to *Sons and Lovers* has been taken up by other critics. Diane S. Bonds, in *Language and the Self in D. H. Lawrence* (UMI Research Press, 1988), partly reprinted in *New Casebooks Sons and Lovers* (ed. Rick Rylance, Macmillan Press, 1997), also reflects on what she terms 'the narrator's shiftiness' in *Sons and Lovers* in addition to dealing with the sexual politics of the text. Barbara Shapiro, in her paper 'Transitional States and Psychic Change' in *Contemporary Psychoanalysis* (January, 1999), discusses the way in which the boundaries between characters and narrator are blurred in Lawrence. She draws an analogy here between Lawrence and Dostoevsky, quoting Bakhtin's comments about the

KEYWORD

Dialogic: was a term used by the Soviet critic Mikhail Bakhtin in his writings on language. He described Dostoevsky's novels as being in the dialogic form, by which he meant that the characters in them speak in a variety of independent voices, not subject to the authoritative control of the author. He contrasted this with Tolstoy's narrative method, where the author does exert such control.

dialogic nature of Dostoevsky's writing which she feels applies equally well to Lawrence.

Nicholas Marsh

Nicholas Marsh's *D. H. Lawrence: The Novels* (Macmillan Press, 2000), examines *Sons and Lovers, The Rainbow* and *Women in Love*. Although there are chapters dealing with Lawrence's life, his place in the development of the novel and the views of other critics, the author concentrates principally on the three novels under discussion by a careful and considered examination of the language used in them. Marsh is particularly helpful when discussing what he calls Lawrence's 'incremental style'. He sees Lawrence as a psychological writer struggling to convey nuances of meaning through 'lists of successive words or phrases, each one qualifying, modulating or contributing to the sense Lawrence wants to convey.' He analyses the way in which the texture of language used and the patterning of sentences follows the movement of a character's thoughts and helps us to understand a great deal about them. Each of the first five chapters concludes with a 'suggested work' section, especially useful for the newcomer to Lawrence. The reader is encouraged to use the close analyses and ideas of the chapter to progress his or her study of the novels along structured guidelines.

Marsh studies male/female relationships and emotions in these novels, looking at psychology and gender characteristics. He deals with class and society, including reference to Lawrence's social and political ideas. For him these are aspects which merit consideration when examining the narrative structure, imagery and symbolism of the novels. This he does consummately well, being clear without being patronizing. If you only read one other book on Lawrence, make it this one.

Helen Baron

In a paper entitled 'Disseminated Consciousness in *Sons and Lovers*', to be found in *Essays in Criticism* (October, 1998), Helen Baron looks at the way Lawrence's unusual use of syntax and vocabulary 'dissolves the barriers separating individuals from each other and probes the problematic relationship between identity and consciousness.' Her focused, intelligent approach is not dissimilar to Marsh's.

In her paper, Baron analyses a series of short extracts from the novel to illustrate her argument. One, which will serve as an example here, is the episode where the pregnant Mrs Morel is in her garden, succumbing to 'a kind of swoon' in the moonlight. Baron quotes two brief excerpts from the passage and points the 'multiple vocabulary of melting and mixing and the strings of "s" and "m" sounds, as well as the unusual syntax.' She examines the latter most carefully, pointing out, for instance, that Lawrence's use of 'her consciousness *in* the child' (my italics), rather than the more usual and expected 'of', gives 'the impression that within Mrs Morel's totality her "self" and her "consciousness" are separate parts which live in an undefined relationship to each other'.

Later in the essay, Baron uses Lawrence's language to argue that this experience was formative for Paul:

> In the presentation of Paul's unusual capacity for perceptions and sensations, Lawrence seems constantly to take his bearings from the ante-natal experience he had invented for Paul of sharing in his mother's swoon, when 'her self melted out like scent' and the 'child too melted with her in the mixing-pot of moonlight'.

This fine-tuned sensibility is something which the adult Paul can access and plumb as an artist.

✳ ✳ ✳ *SUMMARY* ✳ ✳ ✳

- Leavis revolutionizes attitudes to Lawrence, focusing attention away from the man to the text.

- Early polemic feminist critics were followed by those of a more balanced view.

- More recent feminist views include wider reference to other academic interests.

- Marxist/materialist approaches to Lawrence are radically different.

- Recent criticism by Marsh and Baron redresses the balance.

READ MORE NOVELS AND NOVELLAS BY LAWRENCE

Lawrence was an extraordinarily versatile writer who covered a lot of ground in his relatively short life – both in terms of genre and amount written. You may wish to read more of his novels; if you have not already sampled his short stories or slightly longer novellas such as *The Fox* then try them at the first opportunity.

Although it is very much Lawrence's fiction which dominates the foreground in people's minds when they think of him as an author, he was also, as we have seen, a poet of some stature – and a hugely successful writer of non-fiction. There is thus plenty of choice when considering where to go next. Lawrence's plays are well worth looking at – and seeing performed, of course, if you can. His non-fiction, essays, travel-writing and letters are both enjoyable and rewarding. They also tell you a great deal about Lawrence himself.

READ HIS PLAYS

Lawrence wrote eight plays, only three of which were published and two performed in his life-time. The contemporary London stage was not ready for him: it was dogged by philistinism and snobbery. More surprisingly, in view of their quality, they are not often performed today – perhaps because television has provided plenty in the way of working-class realism; they seem less original.

This is a pity, because Lawrence's gift for dialogue positively flowers in his plays; he is also a master of silences. George Bernard Shaw, not usually given to praise of other dramatists, was particularly impressed by what he referred to as the 'vividly effective dialogue' in a performance of *The Widowing of Mrs Holroyd* which he saw in 1926. However, the dialogue is not the only strength. Characters such as Mrs Purdy and Mrs Gascoigne in *The Daughter-in-Law* are compelling and completely credible, the regional rhythms of their dialect having a poetic force. Their speech contains occasional sharp, salty proverbs – the meaning of which has clearly been exemplified in their own experience – the bitter conviction of their truth gives poignancy to the characters. Several of Lawrence's early plays, like this one or *A Collier's Friday Night*, share the Oedipal theme of *Sons and Lovers*. You can access these scripts in *D. H. Lawrence: The Plays* (ed. Schwarze and Worthen, Cambridge University Press, 1999).

STUDY HIS ESSAYS

Some of Lawrence's essays are frequently referred to by critics as a reference point for his ideas. If you wish to fully appreciate the line of argument put forward by these critics, you, too, will need to read the essays. The 'Study of Thomas Hardy' in *The Study of Thomas Hardy and Other Essays* (ed. Bruce Steele, Cambridge University Press, 1985) is one of these. This is not because Lawrence's ideas on Hardy are strikingly definitive but because Lawrence used the opportunity which writing on Hardy gave him to launch off into directions which interested him. This is fairly typical of Lawrence; it means that the essay titles are not always overly helpful as a guide to content. For instance, his essay on Benjamin Franklin in *Selected Essays* includes a very inspiring and imaginatively worded 'creed' of Lawrence's own: as usual one learns at least as much about Lawrence as the ostensible subject of the essay.

Lawrence's essays are interesting for their stimulating ideas and the startling, vivid beauty of their descriptions. 'Her bubble of frail, pale, pure gold rests on the round frill of her green collar' he says of the flowering winter aconite. He describes the terracing on precipitous slopes in Italy as 'little shelves of earth, where already the grey olive stands semi-invisible, and the grape-vine twists upon its own scars.' Both these are from 'Flowery Tuscany', also in *Selected Essays* (Penguin, 1965).

INDULGE IN HIS TRAVEL WRITING

Essays such as 'Flowery Tuscany' are a tribute to Lawrence's ability to describe places with a joyous freshness. You may well also enjoy a full-length piece like *Sea and Sardinia*. This was a product of a brief stay there in January 1921.

Sea and Sardinia is Lawrence at the top of his form. Quite apart from the insight it gives into travelling in the 1920s before tourism and back-packing as we now know it, (Lawrence's 'knapsack' is an object of local fascination and suspicion) there are the usual brilliantly encapsulated and memorable descriptive details of people, produce, places and landscapes. Then there is the attractive style of the thing: the flowing lyricism; the wry caricatures; the exaggeration for comic effect and the tongue-in-cheek understatement. Lawrence makes a delightful guide on this excursion – as John Worthen has said in his introduction to the Penguin edition (1999), 'Self-disclosure, self-parody and vulnerable honesty make the narrator a sympathetic character, despite his eruptions of temper.'

STUDY HIS LETTERS

Lawrence was a prolific correspondent; his letters are a good way to get the feel of the man he was. Like anyone, he writes from very different moods at different times and he adjusts the style and content to different recipients. His letters make entertaining reading: he gallops through a gamut of subjects – from the aside that he is currently mending his own underwear to a deliciously catty opinion cast out with seeming casualness on James Joyce: 'Nothing but old fags and cabbage-stumps of quotations from the Bible and the rest, stewed in the juice of deliberate, journalistic dirty-mindedness.' (To Maria and Aldous Huxley, 15 August, 1928.) Even Lawrence's invective is delivered with a sense of joyous relish.

Lawrence has now had his surviving letters printed in full, in the Cambridge edition published from 1979 to 1993. You may find it most satisfactory to dip in to these – at least you can choose to read and skip material as you will, whereas if you choose one of the edited versions of his letters, someone else will have done the selection process for you.

Not even the Cambridge edition is definitively complete, of course, because Lawrence and some of his recipients either deliberately destroyed or did not keep correspondence. Only one letter from Lawrence to his mother survives. Jessie Chambers destroyed all the letters which Lawrence wrote her – although she did publish excerpts from these in her memoir *D. H. Lawrence: A Personal Record* (Cambridge University Press, 1980).

OTHER PERSPECTIVES
Jessie Chambers's account is particularly interesting to read as an additional perspective on events of Lawrence's life which he drew on to write *Sons and Lovers*. Frieda's account of their life together in *Not I, But the Wind* (Granada, 1983), provides another slant on the married life of the Lawrences.

There are several biographies of Lawrence in print. One of the most comprehensive is Brenda Maddox's *The Married Man: A Life of D. H. Lawrence* (Vintage, 1998). This has the inestimable advantage of being very readable as well as providing shrewd insights and careful research. Alternatively, you might find it more convenient to look up

John Worthen's very sound biography which is available on the University of Nottingham's Lawrence Website.

The following search engines all offer a good selection of Lawrence links: Google, Infind, Northern Light, Dogpile, C4, Surfwax. The Ramanim Society is an e-mail group which you can contact to discuss Lawrence's life and works. If you are interested in films, try Lawrence filmography; the Sean Bean website will give you further details of Ken Russell's production of 'Lady Chatterley.' Eastwood and D. H. Lawrence offers a virtual tour of places with Lawrence connections. If you are able to visit the area, go to the D. H. Lawrence Birthplace Museum at Eastwood and the National Mining Museum at Caphouse Colliery, Wakefield. The D. H. Lawrence Society, based in Eastwood, publishes a twice-yearly newsletter and an annual journal. You can get details of their programme from the Alliance of Literary societies.

* * *SUMMARY* * *

● There are plenty of novels, novellas and short stories to enjoy.

● Lawrence's plays demonstrate his sharp ear for dialogue.

● His essays are interesting in themselves and for what they reveal about the author.

● Travel-writing and letters disclose Lawrence's wit as well as his intolerances.

● Biography and websites can be useful sources of information.

GLOSSARY

Alliteration Repetition of the same sounds, usually the initial consonants of words, or stressed syllables in neighbouring words, for special effect, for example the murmuring of innumerable bees.

Bildungsroman A novel of personal development.

Blutbrüderschaft This means 'blood-brotherhood'. Two men who were actually unrelated would swear to act as brothers towards each other. This does not imply any sexual relationship.

Catharsis This is a term used by Aristotle in his *Poetics*. The translation literally means 'purgation'. Aristotle developed the idea that great tragic drama had certain characteristics, one of which was that it would arouse tremendously strong emotions of pity and fear in the spectator. Watching the play would have a therapeutic effect on the audience, who would leave the theatre at the end of the performance purged of these emotions.

Dialogic was a term used by the Soviet critic Mikhail Bakhtin in his writings on language. He described Dostoevsky's novels as being in the dialogic form, by which he meant that the characters in them speak in a variety of independent voices, not subject to the authoritative control of the author. He contrasted this with Tolstoy's narrative method, pointing out that this author did exert such control.

Ego A Freudian term used to mean that part of the mind which is in touch with outer reality and in conscious control of inner impulses. This is opposed to the id, which Freud used to describe unconscious forces

Feminism Feminism in literature focuses on the experience of women, particularly in the novel. A feminist approach to *Sons and Lovers* finds gender and sexuality to be the guiding principles in the novel.

Free verse Now a very common form of writing, characterized by a lack of formal structure, a freedom from rigid metrical patterns, and often with no formal rhyming patterns. This does not necessarily imply that that there are no formal devices used in the verse, simply that they do not conform to a traditional pattern – they are often unique to a particular poem.

Könstlerroman This is a particular version of a novel of personal development, where the novel is about the growth and development of an artist, for example, *David Copperfield*.

Marxism In literature this indicates that the writer is writing from the standpoint of Marx's philosophical ideas which take the class struggle to be fundamental to history. Thus a Marxist interpretation of *Sons and Lovers* will focus on the difference of social class between Paul's parents as an explanation for his difficulties and attitudes.

Myth A myth is a fiction concerned with creation and explains how something came to exist. James Joyce relied on mythical material in *Ulysses*.

Oedipal This refers to what is known as an Oedipus complex. This important idea in Freudian psychology postulates that a small boy, around the age of four or five, goes through a stage of feeling possessive, incestuous love for his mother and consequent jealousy of his father. The term gets its name from a well-known play by Sophocles in which Oedipus, separated from his mother at birth, later unknowingly returns to his land of origin to kill his father and marry his mother. The Oedipal period of development should, under normal circumstances, merely be an important but passing stage. If, however, the child becomes fixated on his mother at this point in time it may lead to an inability to form later healthy adult relationships.

Post-structuralism This tends to reveal that the meaning of any text is inherently unstable. It is a rather loose term which refers to the process of deconstructing the text.

Psychoanalytical criticism This stems from Freud's study of personality. The psychoanalytical approach to *Sons and Lovers* will see Paul's Oedipal relationship with his mother as central to the novel.

Symbolism – The word symbol derives from a Greek word which means a sign. Literary symbolism combines an image with a concept.

Chronology of Major Works

1905   Writes first poems.

1907   Writes 'The White Stocking' and begins *A Collier's Friday Night* (1934).

1909   Writes 'Odour of Chrysanthemums' and finishes *A Collier's Friday Night*. Poems published in *The English Review*.

1910   Begins writing *The Trespasser* (1912), *Sons and Lovers* (1913), *The Widowing of Mrs Holroyd* (1914).

1911   Writes and publishes *The Married Man, Fight for Barbara* and *The Daughter-in-Law*.

1913   *Love Poems and Others* published. Begins *The Sisters*.

1914   *The Prussian Officer and Other Stories* published. *The Sisters* split and re-written; works on material from this to begin *The Rainbow*. Writes 'Study of Thomas Hardy' (1936).

1915   *The Rainbow* published in September; suppressed in October; prosecuted and banned in November.

1916   *Women in Love* (1920) written, *Twilight in Italy* published.

1917   *Women in Love* rejected by publishers. Begins *Studies in Classic American Literature* (1923) and *Aaron's Rod* (1922). *Look! We Have Come Through!* published.

1918   *New Poems* published. Writes *Touch-and-Go* (1920).

1920   *Women in Love* published in New York. *The Widowing of Mrs Holroyd* first performed. Writes *Psychoanalysis and the Unconscious* (1921), *The Lost Girl* (1920), *Mr Noon* (1984) and many poems from *Birds, Beasts and Flowers* (1923).

1921   Writes *Sea and Sardinia* (1921), *Movements in European History,* finishes *Aaron's Rod* (1922). Puts together collection of short stories, *England, My England* (1922) and three novellas: *The Ladybird, The Fox* and *The Captain's Doll* (1923).

1922   Writes *Kangaroo* (1923) and *Studies in Classic American Literature* (1923).

1923   Writes *The Boy in The Bush* (1924).

1924   Writes *St Mawr,* 'The Woman Who Rode Away', 'The Princess', also most of *Mornings in Mexico* (1927) and *The Plumed Serpent* (1926).

1925   Compiles *Reflections on the Death of a Porcupine* (1925), writes *David* (1926).

1926   Writes *The Virgin and The Gipsy* (1930), starts *Lady Chatterley's Lover* (1928).

1927   Writes *Sketches of Etruscan Places* (1932).

1928   Publishes *Collected Poems,* writes much of *Pansies* (1929).

1929   Writes *Apocalypse* (1931) and *Last Poems* (1932).

INDEX